S0-AZO-745

Contents

In Love with the Church

SAINT JOSEMARÍA ESCRIVÁ

In Love with the Church

 Scepter

IN LOVE WITH THE CHURCH
Translated from *Amar a la Iglesia* (Madrid: Ediciones Palabra, 1986)

Translation, Introduction, Footnotes, and Indices are copyright ©
Fundación Studium, Madrid, and are used with permission.

To learn more about St. Josemaría Escrivá and Opus Dei,
go to www.josemariaescriva.info and www.escrivaworks.org.

First English edition published 1989, Scepter Ltd., London

This edition copyright © 2007
Scepter Publishers Inc., New York
www.scepterpublishers.org
All rights reserved

ISBN 978-1-59417-058-4
Typeset in ITC Garamond fonts

Printed in the United States of America

Prologue

Monsignor Josemaría Escrivá's Love for the Church

By Alvaro del Portillo, Prelate of Opus Dei

In a homily preached in 1963, Monsignor Josemaría Escrivá recalled: "When Pope John XXIII closed the first session of the Second Vatican Council and announced that the name of Saint Joseph was to be included in the canon of the Mass, a prominent churchman telephoned me to say: '*Rallegramenti!* Congratulations! Listening to the Pope's announcement, I thought immediately of you and of how happy you would be.' And indeed I was happy, for in that conciliar gathering, which represented the whole Church brought together in the Holy Spirit, there was proclaimed the great supernatural value of Saint Joseph's life, the value of an ordinary life of work done in God's presence, and in total fulfillment of his will." [1]

The universal call to sanctity

At the request of Pope John XXIII, and afterward of Pope Paul VI, I was called to work as president of the Commission on the Laity in the prepreparatory phase of the Council, and during the Council, as secretary of the Commission on the Discipline of the Clergy and of the Christian People, as well as consultant to four other commissions dealing with important doctrinal and disciplinary matters within the wide range of issues touched upon by the Second Vatican Council. While the results of the work of all these different commissions were being gathered together during the Council's final sessions, I frequently recalled that brief but significant telephone call. So often, in the course of approval of one Council document or another, it would have been a matter of perfect justice to turn to the founder of Opus Dei and to say: "Congratulations! What you have lived in your own soul, and have untiringly taught since 1928, has been proclaimed, with all solemnity, by the Magisterium of the Church!"

Going back in mind and heart to the days of the Council, I can single out two reasons, above all, that led me to say to our Lord: *Gratias tibi Deus, gratias tibi* ("Thank you, O God, thank you!"). The first of these was a vivid recollection from some thirty years earlier. At that time, while I was studying engineering, by the grace of God I received the vocation to Opus Dei, helped by the prayer, mortification, and example of its founder. He helped me to get to grips with my own conscience in a way that gave a new direction to my life as a Christian in the middle of the world, yet with no change of state whatsoever. A great impact was made upon me when I heard from his lips, or read in his writings, statements so simple and so tremendous as: "We have come to say, with the humility of men who know themselves to be sinners and of little importance—*homo peccator sum* ("I am a sinful man") in the words of Saint Peter—but with the faith of persons who allow themselves to be guided by the hand of God, that sanctity is not something for a privileged few. Our Lord calls all men, and from all he expects love: from all, no matter what their state, their profession, or their occupation in life." [2] Elsewhere, in *The Way*, a book of spirituality published in 1939 as an expanded version of his *Consideraciones espirituales* (first published in 1934), Monsignor Escrivá insisted on this point with great conviction: "Your duty is to sanctify yourself. Yes, even you. Who thinks that this task is only for priests and religious? To everyone, without exception, our Lord said: Be perfect, as my heavenly Father is perfect." [3]

This doctrine of the universal call to sanctity was deeply felt in the heart of the founder of Opus Dei, and he repeated it continually, despite the possibility, or even the certainty, that those who had a narrow (some would say monopolistic) vision of the fullness of Christian life, might not understand him very well at all. "From the beginning of the Work in 1928," he wrote some years ago, "I have preached that sanctity is not something for privileged individuals. We have to make it known that all the paths of the earth, all states in life, all professions and honest tasks can be divine." [4]

With the passing of time and through the generosity of the founder of Opus Dei, through his faithful correspondence to divine grace, these teachings have spread throughout the entire world. (By 1965, more than two million copies of *The Way* had already been printed in twelve languages.) Above all, they had become truths firmly implanted in the daily lives of hundreds of thousands of Christians who were either members of Opus Dei or in regular contact with the activities of personal formation organized by the Work.

Hence we can be assured that the Council was fully justified in saying in the Dogmatic Constitution *Lumen gentium*: "It is therefore quite clear that all Christians in any state or walk of life are called to the fullness of Christian life and to the perfection of love." [5] "Accordingly, all Christians, in and through the conditions, duties and circumstances of their life, will sanctify themselves more and more. . . ." [6] "All the faithful are invited and obliged to holiness and the perfection of their own state in life." [7]

The perfect correspondence of Monsignor Escrivá's teaching with that of the Council documents, not only here but also in so many other points, is certainly obvious. I am a witness to the fact that it never passed through his mind to seek the recognition he merited—as so many eminent persons in the Church have already pointed out[8]—as being one of the great forerunners of the Second Vatican Council.

His untiring priestly zeal acted through his richly supernatural and human personality, which was so profoundly warm and communicative. It led him, in the course of more than fifty years as a priest, to deal with hundreds of thousands of persons of all ages and conditions who sought his spiritual counsel and assistance. Since the time of Opus Dei's foundation, he had tirelessly received people singly or in groups. These groups were quite large at times, notably during his trips of *catechesis* (as he liked to call his work) through nearly all of Europe and the Americas. Besides these large-scale get-togethers, there were many others as a constant feature of his daily life, in which non-Catholics and non-Christians from the most varied parts of the globe would come to see him in Rome, where he lived since 1946. "I cannot say 'no,'" he would repeat—while at the same time making sure, and at the cost of notable sacrifice, that this direct priestly work did not in any way jeopardize the other *very direct* priestly task of governing the Work, because he always discovered in his work, that of each moment, the duty of co-redeeming, of seeing souls.

I recall all this because, among the innumerable friends of Monsignor Escrivá there were many bishops from various countries (Council fathers in those years of Vatican II) who benefited from the warmth of his priestly affection—so direct, cordial, and loyal—as well as from the light of a deep interior life and vast pastoral experience. How many were the occasions (I can vouch for them, for I was present at those conversations) on which his life and experience shed light on grave doctrinal and disciplinary problems, all the while respecting with delicate reserve the workings of the Council.

This huge priestly capacity to give of himself ("I cannot say 'no'") was always accompanied by a careful effort *to hide and to disappear*, to avoid any of the multiple forms in which the subtle temptations of personal affirmation can disguise themselves, even in apostolic work. In 1934 he had written: "To shine like a star . . . the desire to be a high burning flame in the heavens? Better to be like a torch that burns hidden but igniting all that it touches. This is your apostolate; this is why you have been placed here on earth."[9] Many years later, in 1975, when he was about to celebrate the fiftieth anniversary of his priesthood, he told us, his children: "I don't want you to prepare a solemn affair, because I want to spend this anniversary in accordance with my usual practice: my role is to hide and disappear, so that only Jesus stands out." I cannot but confess that my heart was filled with joy, together with that serene sorrow which faith gives to those who have been separated from the ones whom they love, when I was able to reread in some of his early papers the same intention expressed in the very same words, written with quick and well-defined strokes: "to hide myself and disappear."

The Second Vatican Council ended its last session more than ten years ago, and has become a part of history. Monsignor Escrivá continues to live, but now he is in Heaven; and despite his wishes, it is no longer possible for him to hide himself, because "A city cannot be hidden if it is built on a mountain-top."[10] Although extensive and detailed studies will be needed to tap all of the doctrinal wealth, both theoretical and practical, which the Founder of Opus Dei has brought to the living body of the Church, I think that it is well worth mentioning here, even if it be only in summary fashion, some particular points, "because it is a glorious thing to proclaim the works of God,"[11] works which the Lord has carried out in making use of an instrument that was "good and faithful."[12]

The priestly soul: the universal call to apostolate

If one were to describe the core of the Second Vatican Council's teaching and its overall thought, a place would be given to the concept of the Church as "a people brought into unity from the unity of the Father, the Son, and the Holy Spirit," [13] according to an expression of Saint Cyprian in the Council's Constitution *Lumen gentium*. The united people, the Mystical Body of Christ, extends the redemptive and sanctifying action of the Head to the end of time. It does so through all of the Catholic faithful, because all of them are called to carry out the great task of bringing men to God, each one in his or her particular circumstances. "The Lord Jesus 'whom the Father consecrated and sent into the world' (John 10:36) makes his whole Mystical Body share in the anointing of the Spirit wherewith He has been anointed: for in that Body all the faithful are made a holy and a kingly priesthood." [14]

When Monsignor Escrivá dealt with this teaching concerning the common priesthood of the faithful, even in the early years of Opus Dei he would remind the members of the Work—laymen with a wide variety of professions and involved in all sorts of secular occupations—that *this priestly soul* was completely compatible with their *lay mentality*. "If the Son of God has become a man and died on the Cross, it was so that all men might be one with him and the Father (see John 17:22). All of us, therefore, are called to form a part of this divine unity. With a priestly soul and with the Holy Mass as the center of our interior life, we strive to be present with Jesus, between God and men." [15] "Through Baptism all of us have been made priests of our lives, 'to offer spiritual sacrifices acceptable to God through Jesus Christ' (1 Pet 2:5), to carry out our every action with a spirit of obedience to God's will and thus to perpetuate the mission of the God-man." [16] This explains the apostolic responsibility of the priestly soul, which feels the divine urging, stemming from Baptism, to co-redeem with Christ.

The Council has reminded us that "Every activity of the Mystical Body with this in view [the spreading of the Kingdom of Christ on earth] is called *apostolate*. The Church realizes it through all her members, though in different ways. In fact, the Christian vocation, of its nature, is a vocation to the apostolate." [17] Within that hierarchical order which the ministerial priesthood establishes and guarantees, the mission of Christ and the Church continues in a mission that corresponds, *ratione Baptismi*,[18] to all the faithful, active members of a living body: "Each disciple of Christ has the obligation of spreading the faith to the best of his ability." [19]

This universal call to the apostolate, inseparably united in the priestly soul to the universal call to sanctity, was another constant point of emphasis in the teaching of Monsignor Escrivá. He always saw the apostolic responsibility of laymen as a divine command, the vital effect produced by sacramental grace, because Christ himself had entrusted to the baptized the duty and the right to dedicate themselves to apostolate. This apostolate is meant to be carried out above all and primarily in and through the very circumstances and the very same secular—not ecclesiastical—structures forming the framework of their everyday lives as citizens and ordinary Christians: "In 1932, commenting for my sons and daughters in Opus Dei on some aspects and consequences of the special dignity and responsibility that Baptism confers upon people, I wrote for them in a document: 'The prejudice that ordinary members of the faithful must limit themselves to assisting the clergy in ecclesiastical apostolates has to be rejected. There is no reason why the secular apostolate should always be a mere participation in the apostolate of the hierarchy. Lay people too have a duty to do apostolate: not because they receive a canonical mission, but because they are a part of the Church. Their mission . . . is fulfilled in their profession, their job, their family, and among their colleagues and friends.'" [20]

The priestly soul—namely, a soul that desires to make the spiritual priesthood it has received actually bear fruit—means an apostolic spirit, a yearning to serve, an effort to turn the most ordinary actions, one's family and social relations, one's ordinary professional work, into the effective occasion of a filial and continuous encounter with God. Monsignor Escrivá was only repeating this call anew when, during his catechesis throughout all of Latin America, he stated: "Christ is always passing by; passing, but with the desire to stay." We Christians live with an obligation to communicate to all men the fact that Christ is always passing by our side, desiring to travel together with each one of us along the very same path. And he wishes, if we listen to him, to remain with us as on that marvelous afternoon in Emmaus.

I recall one of the last delicate gestures of our Lord toward his servant, Josemaría Escrivá: the last words he spoke in public, only two hours before his departure for Heaven, dealt with that priestly soul which is common to all Christians. It was a confirmation of what he had constantly preached. These words were spoken in a university center, in Castelgandolfo, under the direction of the Women's Section of Opus Dei. He was speaking there to women students from twenty-one countries, from Australia to Poland, from the Philippines to Kenya. He said to them: "Because you are Christians, you have a priestly soul. I tell you this whenever I come here. Your brothers who are laymen also have a priestly soul. You are able to act, and you ought to act, with that priestly soul. And thus, with the grace of God and the ministerial priesthood which we priests of the Work have, we will carry out an efficacious apostolate."

The sanctification of work

"Since it is characteristic of the layman's state in life to live in the midst of the world and secular occupations, laymen are called by God so that, moved by a Christian spirit, they exercise their apostolate in the world, acting like leaven." [21] These considerations of the Decree *Apostolicam actuositatem* are closely linked to a text of the Constitution *Gaudium et spes* in which the Second Vatican Council, expressly referring to the "ordinary tasks" of men, declares that Christians "can rightly look upon their work as a prolongation of the work of the Creator, a service to their fellow men, and their personal contribution to the fulfillment in history of the divine plan." [22]

Monsignor Escrivá emphasized, day after day, that the work of man is a sanctifiable reality and an instrument of one's own sanctification and that of others. "What I have always taught, over the last forty years, is that a Christian should do all honest human work, be it intellectual or manual, with the greatest perfection possible: with human perfection (professional competence) and with Christian perfection (for love of God's will and as a service to mankind). Human work done in this manner, no matter how humble or insignificant it may seem, helps to shape the world in a Christian way. The world's divine dimension is made more visible and our human labor is thus incorporated into the marvelous work of creation and redemption. It is raised to the order of grace. It is sanctified and becomes God's work, *operatio Dei, opus Dei.*" [23]

He liked to present this theological truth, laden with meaning, in graphic terms, readily understandable by all: "Bring Christ into all those places where mankind's varied tasks are being carried out—into the factory, the laboratory, the farm, the craftsman's workshop, the streets of the great cities, and the mountain trails." [24] To work in the presence of

God is a continuous and direct apostolate because in this way Christians can "speak of divine things in the very same language which men use . . . , see God from the very same secular and lay angle from which they deal, or could deal, with the transcendental questions of their lives." [25]

Prayer, work, and apostolate come together in the ordinary existence of Christians, who must overcome the temptation "to lead a kind of double life: on the one hand, an inner life, a life of relationship with God; and on the other, as something separate and distinct, their professional, social and family lives, made up of small earthly realities. No. We cannot lead a double life. We cannot have a split personality if we want to be Christians. There is only one life, made of flesh and spirit. And it is that life which has to become, in both body and soul, holy and filled with God." [26] These words, spoken in 1967, were one more echo of others he had written back in 1943: "We must flee from falsely seeing the spiritual life as nothing more than a restriction of freedom, doctrinal formation as a mere collection of obscure formulas, and apostolate as a kind of extra part-time job to fill one's spare hours." [27] Since 1928, the founder of Opus Dei had been repeating, in the midst of the Church, that truth, which is as "old as the gospel and like the gospel new." It is the truth that one can sanctify oneself and evangelize (if I may use the expression) "one's home ground." Therefore, no gap or separation can exist between what is Christian and what is human, because history allows no other course than that which the salvific designs of God have traced.

Monsignor Escrivá presented this *normality* of the Christian life in a crystal-clear way: "We are ordinary men and women, ordinary Christians, which is enough of a title." [28] Many thousands of men and women, of all races and social backgrounds, have, upon acquiring this new awareness, experienced that they were indeed going along "the divine paths of the earth." Without show, without ostentation, without a lot of noise, as men and women who are in the world by right and vocation, they are born to the life of grace for the purpose of sanctifying all earthly realities. "Have you ever stopped to think how absurd it is to leave one's Catholicism aside on entering a university, a professional association, a cultural society, or Parliament, like a man leaving his hat at the door?" [29]

Freedom and the personal responsibility of Christians

The Second Vatican Council has emphasized that a principal part of the laity's apostolic mission consists in enlivening the diverse environments of the world with a Christian spirit, so as to establish in these sectors of society—professional, social, economic, and so on—that order which is willed by God. Lay people should have the conviction that it is here, in these very circles, that they are directly and immediately involved in the effort to channel all things to Christ.[30] At the same time the Council has pointed out that laymen should carry out their tasks with freedom and personal responsibility: that is to say, with a conscience well formed through a due knowledge of the moral principles which the hierarchy of the Church teaches and interprets.[31] But this can never justify that laymen consider themselves, or act in the diverse questions and specific problems of the temporal order, as a kind of *longa manus* (long arm) of the hierarchy. "It is their task to cultivate a properly informed conscience and to impress the divine law on the affairs of the earthly city. For guidance and spiritual strength, let them turn to the clergy; but let them realize that their pastors will not always be so expert as to have a ready answer to every problem (even every grave problem) that arises. This is not the role of the clergy. It is, rather, up to the laymen to shoulder their responsibilities under the guidance of Christian wisdom and with eager attention to the teaching authority of the Church." [32]

It is therefore not at all strange, but rather quite logical, that together with united adherence to moral principles, there be found a legitimate pluralism among Catholic laymen as regards free personal actions in matters of a professional, social, or political nature. Catholic doctrine does not seek to create dogmas in what are essentially matters of opinion. The mind of the Council clearly supports this view. There was much less support, however—in fact, there was opposition in certain sectors of both civil and ecclesiastical life—when, in 1932, Monsignor Escrivá wrote to the first members of Opus Dei: "Avoid that abuse which seems to be widely intensified in our time—it is manifest in nations throughout the world—which betrays a desire contrary to the legitimate freedom of men, in attempting to oblige all to form a single group in matters of opinion, to turn temporal doctrines into dogmas." [33]

In line with this subject, the Council has reminded us that "very often the Christian vision of some members of the laity will suggest a certain solution in some given situation. Yet it happens rather frequently, and legitimately so, that some of the faithful, with no less sincerity, will see the problem quite differently. Now if one or other of the proposed solutions is too easily associated with the gospel message, they must remember that in those cases no one is permitted to identify the authority of the Church exclusively with his own opinion." [34] Here we have the freedom and personal responsibility of Christians, which Monsignor Escrivá so abundantly preached in order to help Catholics avoid the danger of "belittling their faith" and "reducing it to a human ideology." [35] "A man who knows that the world—and not only the Church—is the place where he finds Christ, loves that world.

He endeavors to become properly trained, intellectually and professionally. He makes up his own mind, in full freedom, about the problems of the environment in which he moves, and he makes his own decisions in consequence. As the decisions of a Christian, they derive from personal reflection, which strives in all humility to grasp the will of God in both the unimportant and the important events of his life. But it never occurs to such a Christian to think or say that he was stepping down from the temple into the world to represent the Church, or that his solutions are *the Catholic solutions* to the problems." [36]

Matrimony: a Christian vocation

God wants the majority of Christians to start a family, with its origin in matrimony, the *sacramentum magnum*.[37] It was not many years ago that many people—and perhaps their prejudice has not yet altogether disappeared—thought that there were only two possible courses to follow in order to achieve sanctity: either the religious life or the priesthood. By either of these paths, the only paths for which a *vocation* would be necessary, one could easily arrive at sanctity. On the other hand, in matrimony, living in the world, one remained in a state far from holiness, because earthly concerns, and in particular the duties related to married life, one's profession, and one's family, would always represent an obstacle to the fullness of Christian life, except in extraordinary cases.

In this context it is easy to appreciate what Monsignor Escrivá, who was at the same time a great defender and promoter of the merits of apostolic celibacy in its different forms, had written in 1939. Recognizing that he was going against what was considered to be the normal view, he wrote: "You laugh because I tell you that you have 'a vocation for marriage'? Well, you have just that: a vocation." [38]

This is something we have no trouble understanding now, but again I repeat that this was not the case at the time. There was no shortage of false teachers who were able to find in these words of such transparent meaning, a starting point for heresy, a position unfaithful to the teaching of the Church. Later, in one of his homilies, Monsignor Escrivá made a summary of what he had taught since the '20s. "Husband and wife are called to sanctify their married life and to sanctify themselves in it. It would be a serious mistake if they were to exclude family life from their spiritual development. The marriage union, the care and education of the children, the effort to provide for the needs of the family as well as for its security and development, the relationships with other persons who make up the community: all these are among the ordinary human situations which Christian couples are called upon to sanctify." [39]

In the fifty years of his priesthood, the founder of Opus Dei brought into thousands of homes this truth, which the Church has also proclaimed in one of the Council's documents: "Authentic married love is raised up by divine love and is directed and enriched by the redemptive power of Christ." [40] With immense joy, I myself have been able to see how a multitude of families throughout the world have received this clarifying light of the Council as a confirmation of what they were already practicing, moved by those warmly supernatural affirmations of Monsignor Escrivá. Many years before the Council, he had presented to them a Christian style of life, identical with that of the first followers of Christ: "Families no different from other families of those times, but living with a new spirit, which spread to all those who were in contact with them. This is what the first Christians were, and this is what we have to be: sowers of peace and joy, the peace and joy that Jesus has brought to us." [41]

The priesthood and sanctity

The spirituality that Monsignor Escrivá sought to spread throughout the Church addresses itself to all the Christian faithful who live in the midst of the world. It is also, therefore, directed toward diocesan priests, members of the faithful who, having received a specific sacrament, that of Holy Orders, can "offer the Holy Sacrifice and forgive sins" and "exercise publicly the priestly office on behalf of men and in the name of Christ." [42]

It is clear, then, that the priest cannot be a bureaucrat, someone who preaches sanctity but does not himself strive for it. In a text of Monsignor Escrivá's written in 1945, we read: "As demanded by their common Christian vocation, both priests and laymen, by reason of the one baptism which they have received, must equally aspire to sanctity, which is a participation in the divine life [see Saint Cyril of Jerusalem, *Catechesis*, 21, 2]. The sanctity to which they are called is not greater in the priest than in the layman, since the latter is not called to be a second-class Christian. Holiness, both in the priest and in the layman, is nothing other than the perfection of Christian life, the fullness of divine filiation." [43]

I can vouch for the fact that, when these expressions made their entry into those quarters where the documents of the Second Vatican Council were being prepared and studied, they at first caused considerable surprise. Later, they found total acceptance. They were a decisive factor in doing away with a *statist* view of the life and ministry of the diocesan priest, in which his call to sanctity was seen only in terms of his state, that is, as *superior* to that of the laity and *inferior* to that of the religious priest. The decree *Presbyterorum ordinis* manifestly proclaimed what Monsignor Escrivá had taught: "Like all Christians, they [the priests] have already received in the consecration of Baptism the sign and the gift of their great calling and grace. So they are enabled and obliged, even in the midst of human weakness, to seek perfection, according to the words of our Lord: You, therefore, must be perfect, as your heavenly Father is perfect (Matt 5:48)." [44]

"The priests will be able to contribute effectively to each one's knowing how to discover in the events of life, whether great or small, the proper way to act and the will of God." [45]

I was moved by the parallel between these lines I have just quoted and a homily that Monsignor Escrivá preached in 1960: "If my own personal experience is of any help, I can say that I have always seen my work as a priest and shepherd of souls as being aimed at helping each person to face up to all the demands of his life and to discover what God wants of him in particular." [46] This is not the place for a detailed study, but such parallelisms with the Council arise in many other aspects of Monsignor Escrivá's teaching on the priestly life and ministry: the need, for instance, to develop human virtues also in order to have a sacerdotal spirituality;[47] the importance of being an instrument of unity among the faithful, avoiding the temptation to belittle the Faith by aligning oneself with ideologies and human factions that divide men;[48] the possibility and suitability of well-ordered associations that would assist priests to attain sanctity through the exercise of their own ministry;[49] the unity and harmony between interior life and pastoral activity which a priest can achieve when he finds in the Holy Sacrifice of the Mass "the center and root" of his existence;[50] the need for personal prayer, frequent confession, and maintaining traditional practices of piety recommended by the long experience of the Church;[51] the importance of the priest's seeing clearly that the exercise of his ministry—his "ordinary work"—is precisely the occasion and irreplaceable means for achieving sanctity,[52] and so on.

I would like to add here what is but one more among

many vivid memories bearing on this theme: namely, the authentic joy with which the founder of Opus Dei, an untiring preacher of the need to be "contemplatives in the middle of the world," read the following paragraph from the Constitution *Lumen gentium*, which answers the objections that the cares and concerns of the priestly ministry could be obstacles for seeking personal sanctity: "Rather than be held back by perils and hardships in their apostolic labors, they [priests] should rise to greater holiness, nourishing and fostering their action with an overflowing contemplation, for the nourishment of the entire Church of God."[53]

Ecumenism

I have already mentioned the fact that many non-Catholics and also non-Christians benefited from Monsignor Escrivá's unlimited capacity for human friendship and from his priestly attention, two facets which were always inseparably united in his conduct. These persons had either come to speak with him in private, or they had addressed him in public, asking him questions or seeking advice during his numerous gatherings of catechesis with groups of men and women of all ages, social backgrounds, and religious denominations. On all of these occasions, his loyalty to the one Church of Jesus Christ, together with his delicate respect for the "freedom of individual consciences" (which he carefully distinguished from the inadmissible "freedom of conscience"), led him to carry out a direct and extremely fruitful ecumenical work or apostolate *ad plenitudinem fidei* (bringing them to the fullness of the faith) with thousands of souls. And all of this long before the word "ecumenism" itself had made its entry into common ecclesiastical parlance.

When, back in 1967, a journalist asked him how Opus Dei fitted into the overall picture of ecumenism, Monsignor

Escrivá answered with his habitual good humor: "Last year I told a French journalist—and I know that the anecdote has been retold, even in publications of our separated brethren—that I once told the Holy Father John XXIII, moved by the affable and fatherly kindness of his manner: 'Holy Father, in our Work all men, Catholics or not, have always found a welcome. I have not learned ecumenism from your Holiness.' He laughed, for he knew that way back in 1950, the Holy See had authorized Opus Dei to accept into the Association, as Cooperators, people who are not Catholics or even Christians." [54]

Monsignor Escrivá then went on to single out, on the subject of ecumenism, numerous repercussions of the spirituality characteristic of the Institution he had founded: "In fact, there are many separated brethren who feel attracted by the spirit of Opus Dei and who cooperate in our apostolates, and they include ministers and even bishops of their respective confessions. As contacts increase, we receive more and more proofs of affection and cordial understanding. And it is because members of Opus Dei center their spirituality simply on trying to love responsibly the commitments and demands of Christian Baptism. A desire to seek Christian perfection and to do apostolate, endeavoring to sanctify their own professional work; the fact of their living immersed in secular reality and respecting its proper autonomy, but dealing with it with the spirit and love of contemplative souls; the primacy we give in the organization of our apostolate to the individual, to the action of the Spirit upon souls, to the dignity and freedom that derive from the divine filiation of Christians; the defense of the legitimate freedom of initiative, within a necessary respect for the common good, against the monolithic and institutionalistic conception of the apostolate of the laity: these and other aspects of our way of being and acting are so many points of easy contact with our separated brethren. Here they find, put into living practice, a good many of the doctrinal presuppositions in which they, and we Catholics, have placed so many well-founded ecumenical expectations." [55]

Testimony of love for the Church

The universal call to sanctity and apostolate: baptismal spirituality, love for the world, for all noble human realities and especially for human work, a participation in the creative work of God—together with the love of Christ; the enrichment, both doctrinally and ascetically, of the various demands of the ministerial priesthood; a deepening of the supernatural dimensions of human love and of the Christian family; an ecumenical spirit that reaffirms, with unlimited charity but without errors, the truth that the one Church of Christ is catholic, apostolic, and Roman. But above all, and encompassing all: unconditional dedication to the Church "which prays and works at the same time, so that the entire world be transformed into the people of God, the Body of the Lord and the Temple of the Holy Spirit, and so that in Christ, the Head of all things, honor and glory may be rendered to the Father and Creator of the universe." [56]

These lines have presented only a rapid survey of that sense of the Church which filled the holy soul of Monsignor Escrivá, always at the service of the Church by means of the path of Opus Dei. Our founder and father offered his whole life for the Spouse of Christ, for his Vicar on earth, for all men. His burning words, his heart overflowing with understanding and warmth, continue—and will continue ever more—to inflame the souls of millions of Christians throughout the whole world, leading them to sacrifice themselves joyfully so that the most loving will of God "that all men be saved and come to the full knowledge of the truth" [57] may come to be realized.

In Love with
the Church

Loyalty to the Church

A homily given on June 4, 1972

The texts of this Sunday's liturgy form a chain of invocations 1
to the Lord. We tell him that he is our support, our rock, our
defense.[1] The Collect also takes up the theme of the Introit:
"You never refuse your light to those who stand fast in the
firmness of your love."[2]

In the Gradual we continue to have recourse to him: "In
my distress I cry to the Lord. . . . Deliver me, O Lord, from
wicked lips, from a deceitful tongue. O Lord, in thee do I take
refuge."[3] We are moved by the insistence of God our Father,
who is determined to remind us that we ought to appeal to
his mercy, always, no matter what happens. Now as well, at a
time in which confused voices are rending the Church, many
souls are going astray because they do not find good shepherds, other Christs, who would guide them to the Lord of
Love. They find, instead, "thieves and robbers" who come "to
steal and kill and destroy."[4]

Let us not be afraid. The Church, which is the Body of
Christ must indefectibly be the path and the sheepfold of the
Good Shepherd, the strong foundation and the way open to
all men. We have just read in the Gospel: "Go out to the
highways and hedges, and compel people to come in, so that
my house may be filled."[5]

But what is the Church? Where is the Church? Bewildered 2
and disoriented, many Christians do not find sure answers
to these questions. And they come to believe that perhaps
the answers which the Magisterium has formulated for centuries—and which good catechisms have proposed with
the necessary precision and simplicity—have now been

superseded and must be replaced by new ones. A series of facts and difficulties seem to have come together to darken the bright countenance of the Church. Some maintain that the valid Church can be found only in their personal zeal to accommodate it to what they call *modern times.* Others cry out: the Church is nothing more than man's desire for solidarity. We ought to change it, they say, in accord with present circumstances.

They are wrong. The Church today is the same one Christ founded. It cannot be any other. "The Apostles and their successors are the vicars of God with regard to the rule of the Church as instituted through faith and with regard to the sacraments of the faith. Hence, just as it is not lawful for them to constitute any other Church, so too it is not lawful for them either to hand down any other faith or to institute any other sacraments. Rather, the Church is said to have been built up with the 'sacraments which flowed from the side of Christ hanging on the Cross.' " [6] The Church must be recognized by the four marks in the profession of faith of one of the first Councils, as we pray in the Creed of the Mass: "One, holy, catholic, and apostolic Church." [7]

These are the essential properties of the Church, which are derived from its nature as Christ intended it. And, being essential, they are also marks, signs, which distinguish it from any other human gathering, even though in the others the name of Christ may be pronounced.

A little more than a century ago, Pope Pius IX briefly summed up this traditional teaching: "The true Church of Christ is constituted and recognized, by divine authority, in the four marks which in the creed we affirm as to be believed. And each of these marks is so united with the others that it cannot be separated from them. For this reason, that which truly is catholic and is called Catholic should at the same time shine forth by the prerogatives of unity, of holiness and of apostolic succession." [8] It is, I emphasize, the traditional teaching of the Church, which the Second Vatican Council has repeated again, even though in recent years some may have forgotten it, led by a false ecumenism. "This is the sole Church of Christ which in the Creed we profess to be one, holy, catholic, and apostolic, which our Savior, after his Resurrection, entrusted to Peter's pastoral care, commissioning him and the other Apostles to extend and rule it, and which he raised up for all ages as the pillar and mainstay of the truth." [9]

The Church is one

"That they may be one, even as we are one," [10] Christ cries out to his Father; "that they may all be one; even as thou, Father, art in me and I in thee; that they also may be in us." [11] This exhortation to unity flows in a constant stream from the lips of Jesus, "for every kingdom divided against itself is laid waste, and no city or house divided against itself will stand." [12] It is a teaching which is converted into a vehement desire: "And I have other sheep that are not of this fold; I must bring them also, and they will heed my voice. So there shall be one flock, one shepherd." [13]

What beautiful tones Our Lord uses to express this doctrine! He multiplies words and images so that we may understand it, so that this passion for unity may remain engraved on our souls. "I am the true vine and my Father is the vinedresser. Every branch of mine that bears no fruit, he takes away, and every branch that does bear fruit he prunes that it may bear more fruit. . . . Abide in me, and I in you. As the branch cannot bear fruit by itself unless it abides in the vine, neither can you, unless you abide in me. I am the vine, you are the branches. He who abides in me, and I in him, he it is that bears much fruit, for apart from me you can do nothing." [14]

Do you not see how those who separate themselves from the Church, even though they are full of foliage, quickly dry up, and their very fruits are converted into a living bed of worms? Love the holy, Roman, apostolic Church. One! For as Saint Cyprian writes: "He who reaps elsewhere, outside the Church, dissipates the Church of Christ." [15] And Saint John Chrysostom insists: "Do not separate yourself from the Church. Nothing is stronger than the Church. Your hope is the Church; your salvation is the Church; your refuge is the Church. It is higher than the heavens, and broader than the earth; it never grows old, its vigor is eternal." [16]

To defend the unity of the Church is to live very united to Jesus Christ, who is our vine. How? By growing in fidelity to the perennial Magisterium of the Church: "For the Holy Spirit was promised to the successors of Peter not that they should manifest a new doctrine by his revelation, but rather that with his assistance, they should religiously safeguard and faithfully teach the revelation that was handed down through the Apostles—the deposit of faith." [17] By venerating this Mother of ours without stain, and loving the Roman Pontiff, we will preserve unity.

4   Some say that few men are left in the Church. I would say that if all of us loyally safeguarded Christ's doctrine, our numbers would grow considerably, since God wants his house to be filled. In the Church we discover Christ, who is the Love of our loves. And we should desire for all men our vocation, this intimate joy which intoxicates the soul, the limpid sweetness of the merciful heart of Jesus.

One hears it said that we must be ecumenical. So be it. Nevertheless, I fear that behind some self-styled ecumenical activities there is a hidden fraud: for they are activities which do not lead to the love of Christ, to the true vine. For that reason they lack fruit. I ask our Lord each day to expand my heart, that he may continue to supernaturalize the love he has put in my soul for all men, without distinction of race, nationality, cultural condition, or wealth. I sincerely esteem all men, Catholics or not, those who do believe in something and those who do not. I feel sorry for these unbelievers. But Christ founded only one Church: he has only one Spouse.

The union of all Christians? Yes. Even more: the union of all those who believe in God. But there exists only one true Church. There is no need to rebuild it out of pieces dispersed throughout the world, and it does not need to go through any sort of purification in order to be finally cleansed. "The spouse of Christ cannot be adulterous, for she is incorruptible and pure. Only one house knows and safeguards the inviolability of only one bridal bed with chaste modesty. She preserves us for God, she destines for the kingdom the children she has begotten. Anyone who separates himself from the Church unites himself with an adulterer; he leaves behind the promises of the Church and he who abandons the Church of Christ will not achieve the rewards of Christ." [18]

The Church is holy

Now we can understand better how the unity of the Church 5 leads to her holiness, and how one of the principal aspects of her holiness is that unity centered on the mystery of the one and triune God. "There is one body and one spirit, just as you were called to the one hope that belongs to your call; one Lord, one faith, one baptism; one God and Father of us all, who is above all and through all and in all." [19]

Holiness means none other than union with God; a greater intimacy with the Lord, more sanctity. The Church has been willed and founded by Christ, who carries out in this way the will of the Father; the Spouse of the Son is assisted by the Holy Spirit. The Church is the work of the Blessed Trinity; she is holy and our mother, our Holy Mother the Church. We can admire in the Church one perfection which we could call original, and another final, eschatological. Saint Paul refers to both of them in his letter to the Ephesians. "Christ loved the church and gave himself up for her, that he might sanctify her, having cleansed her by the washing of water with the word, that he might present the church to himself in splendor, without spot or wrinkle or any such thing, that she might be holy and without blemish." [20]

The original and constitutive holiness of the Church can be hidden, but never destroyed, since it is indefectible: "The powers of death shall not prevail against it." [21] It can be veiled from human eyes, as I was saying, in certain moments of obscurity, which can become almost universal. But Saint Peter applies to Christians the title of *gens sancta*,[22] a holy nation. And, being members of a holy nation, all the faithful have received a call to holiness, and they must strive to correspond to grace and to be personally holy. Throughout history and now as well, there have been so many Catholics who have truly sanctified themselves: young and old, single and married, priests and lay people, men and women.

But it happens that the personal sanctity of so many faithful—then and now—is not something externally apparent. Frequently we do not recognize the ordinary people, common and holy, who work and live alongside us. From an earthly viewpoint, what stands out most are sin and unfaithfulness: these are more conspicuous.

6   *Gens sancta*, a holy nation, composed of creatures with infirmities. This apparent contradiction marks an aspect of the mystery of the Church. The Church, which is divine, is also human, for it is made up of men, and men have their defects: *Omnes homines terra et cinis*,[23] we men are dust and ashes.

Our Lord Jesus Christ, who founded the holy Church,

expects the members of this people to strive continually to acquire sanctity. Not all respond loyally to his call. And in the spouse of Christ, at one and the same time, both the marvel of the way of salvation and the miseries of those who take up that way are visible.

"It was one and the same purpose—namely, that of perpetuating on this earth the salutary work of the redemption, which caused the divine Redeemer to give the community of human beings, founded by him, the constitution of a society perfect in its own order, provided with all the juridical and social elements. . . . If something is perceived in the Church which points to the infirmity of our human condition, this is not to be attributed to her juridical constitution, but to the lamentable tendency of individuals toward evil, a tendency which her divine Founder suffers to exist even in the higher members of his Mystical Body, for the testing of the virtue of both flock and pastors, and for the greater merit of Christian faith in all." [24]

This is the reality of the Church here and now. For this reason the holiness of the spouse of Christ is compatible with the existence in her bosom of individuals with defects. "Christ did not will sinners to be excluded from the society he had founded; if therefore some members are spiritually infirm, this is no reason for lessening our love toward the Church, but rather for increasing our compassion toward her members." [25]

It would be a sign of very little maturity if, in view of [7] the defects and miseries in any of those who belong to the Church (no matter how high they may be placed by virtue of their function), anyone should feel his faith in the Church and in Christ lessened. The Church is not governed by Peter, nor by John, nor by Paul; she is governed by the Holy Spirit, and the Lord has promised that he will remain at her side "always, to the close of the age." [26]

Listen to what Saint Thomas Aquinas says, elaborating on this point. He is speaking about receiving the sacraments, which are the cause and sign of sanctifying grace: "He who approaches the sacraments receives the sacrament concerned from the minister of the Church, not as such-and-such an individual, but precisely as a minister of the Church. Hence so long as the Church suffers him to remain in his ministry, one receiving a sacrament from him does not share in his sin, but shares in the life of the Church who publicly recognizes him as minister." [27] When the Lord permits human weakness to appear, our reaction ought to be the same as if we were to see our mother ill or treated with disdain: to love her all the more, to bestow on her a greater manifestation of affection, both external and internal.

If we love the Church, there will never arise in us a morbid interest in airing, as the faults of the Mother, the weaknesses of some of her children. The Church, the spouse of Christ, does not have to intone any *mea culpa*. But we do: *mea culpa, mea culpa, mea maxima culpa*. The only true *mea culpa* is a personal one, not the one which attacks the Church, pointing out and exaggerating the human defects which, in this holy Mother, result from the presence in her of men whose actions can go far astray, but which can never destroy—nor even touch—that which we call the original and constitutive holiness of the Church.

God our Lord has indeed compared the Church to the threshing floor, where the straw is piled together with the wheat from which will come bread for the table and bread for the altar; he has compared the Church to a dragnet *ex omni genere piscium congreganti*,[28] which catches both good and bad fish, the bad ones of which are later thrown away.

8   The mystery of the holiness of the Church—that pristine light which can become obscured by the shadows of human baseness—rejects even the slightest thought of suspicion, of

doubt about the beauty of our Mother. Nor can we tolerate, without protesting, that others should insult her. We cannot seek out in the Church vulnerable points in order to criticize them, as some do who show thereby neither their faith nor their love. I cannot conceive of anyone having true affection for his mother who speaks of her with disdain.

Our Mother is holy, because she was born pure and will continue without blemish for all eternity. If at times we are not able to perceive her fair face, let us wipe clean our own eyes. If we are aware that her voice does not please us, let us remove from our ears any hardness which prevents us from hearing in her tone of voice the whistled beckoning of the loving Shepherd. Our Mother is holy, with the holiness of Christ, to whom she is united in body—which is all of us— and in spirit, which is the Holy Spirit, dwelling also in the hearts of each one of us, if we remain in the grace of God.

Holy, holy, holy, we dare sing to the Church, evoking a hymn in honor of the Blessed Trinity. You are holy, O Church, my Mother, because the Son of God, who is holy, founded you. You are holy because the Father, source of all holiness, so ordained it. You are holy because the Holy Spirit, who dwells in the souls of the faithful, assists you, in order to gather together the children of the Father, who will dwell in the Church of Heaven, the eternal Jerusalem.

The Church is catholic

God "desires all men to be saved and to come to the knowl- 9
edge of the truth. For there is one God and there is one mediator between God and men, the man Christ Jesus, who gave himself as a ransom for all, the testimony to which was borne at the proper time." [29] Jesus Christ instituted only one Church. For this reason the spouse of Christ is one and catholic: universal, for all men.

For many centuries now the Church has been spread throughout the world, and it numbers persons of all races and walks of life. But the universality of the Church does not depend on its geographical distribution, even though this is a visible sign and a motive of credibility. The Church was catholic already at Pentecost. It was born catholic from the wounded heart of Jesus, as a fire which the Holy Spirit enkindled.

In the second century the Christians called the Church catholic in order to distinguish it from the sects which, using the name of Christ, were betraying his doctrine in one way or another. "We call it catholic," writes Saint Cyril, "not because it is spread throughout the world, from one extreme to the other, but because in a universal way and without defect it teaches all the dogmas which men ought to know, of both the visible and the invisible, the celestial and the earthly. Likewise, because it draws to true worship all types of men, those who govern and those who are ruled, the learned and the ignorant. And finally, because it cures and makes healthy all kinds of sins, whether of the soul or of the body, possessing in addition—by whatever name it may be called—all the forms of virtue, in deeds and in words and in every kind of spiritual gift." [30]

The catholicity of the Church does not depend either on whether or not non-Catholics acclaim and acknowledge it. Nor does it have anything to do with the fact that in non-spiritual matters the opinions of some persons in positions of authority in the Church are taken up—and at times exploited—by those who fashion public opinion, when these churchmen have views similar to theirs. It will often happen that the aspect of truth which will be defended in any human ideology will find an echo or foundation in the perennial teaching of the Church. This is, in a certain sense, a sign of the divinity of the revelation which the Magisterium safeguards. But the spouse of Christ is catholic even when it is deliberately ignored by many, and even abused and persecuted, as unfortunately happens in so many places.

The Church is not a political party, or a social ideology, or   10
a worldwide organization for harmony or material progress, even though we recognize the nobility of these and other activities. The Church has always undertaken and undertakes today an immense work on behalf of the needy, of those who suffer, of all those who bear in any way the consequences of the only true evil, which is sin. And to all—to those who are in any way deprived and to those who claim to enjoy the fullness of earthly goods—the Church comes to confirm only one, essential, definitive truth: that our destiny is eternal and supernatural, that only in Jesus Christ are we saved for all time, and that only in him will we achieve in some way already in this life true peace and happiness.

Ask God our Lord now, along with me, that we Catholics may never forget these truths, and that we may resolve to put them into practice. The Catholic Church does not need the approval of men, for it is the work of God.

We will show ourselves to be Catholics by the fruits of sanctity which we produce, for sanctity does not admit of any frontiers, nor is it the patrimony of any particular group. We will show ourselves to be Catholics if we pray, if we strive to direct ourselves to God at all times, if we make an effort always and in all things to be just—in the broadest sense of the term *justice*, which is used frequently in these times with a materialistic and erroneous connotation—if we love and defend the personal freedom of other men.

I remind you also of another sign of the catholicity of the Church: the faithful preservation and administration of the sacraments as they were instituted by Jesus Christ, without human deformations or evil attempts to interpret them psychologically or sociologically. For "it is not for one man to

decide how another shall use what is under the latter's power
and authority. All he can decide is what is under his own
power. Since, therefore, human sanctification lies under the
power of God, who sanctifies, it is not for man to decide of
his own judgment which materials are to be chosen for him
to be sanctified by. This, rather, is something which should be
determined by divine institution." [31]

The attempt to take universality away from the essence of
the sacraments would perhaps be justified if it were only a
matter of *signs*, of symbols, which are subject to the natural
laws of comprehension and understanding. But "the sacraments of the New Law are causes and signs at the same time.
Hence too it is that, as the usual formula puts it, they effect
what they figuratively express. And from this it is also clear
that in them the essential characteristics of a sacrament are
perfectly fulfilled, inasmuch as they are designed for something sacred in the sense not merely of being signs of it but of
being causes of it as well." [32]

11   The Catholic Church is Roman. I savor that word, Roman!
I feel completely Roman, since Roman means universal,
catholic. For it leads me to love tenderly the Pope, *il dolce
Cristo in terra*, as Saint Catherine of Siena, whom I count as a
most beloved friend, liked to repeat.

"From this catholic Roman center," Paul VI emphasized in
the closing stages of the Second Vatican Council, "no one is,
in theory, beyond reach; all can and should be reached. For
the Catholic Church, no one is a stranger, no one is excluded,
no one is to consider himself far away." [33] I venerate with all
my strength the Rome of Peter and Paul, bathed in the blood
of martyrs, the center from which so many have set out to
propagate throughout the world the saving word of Christ.
To be Roman does not entail any manifestation of provincial-
ism, but rather of authentic ecumenism. It presupposes the
desire to enlarge the heart, to open it to all men with the

redemptive zeal of Christ, who seeks all men and takes in all men, for he has loved all men first.

Saint Ambrose wrote a few words which comprise, as it were, a song of joy: "Where Peter is, there is the Church; and where the Church is, not death, but eternal life reigns." [34] For where Peter and the Church are, there Christ is; and he is salvation, the only way.

The Church is apostolic

Our Lord founded the Church on the weakness—but also on the fidelity—of a few men, the Apostles, to whom he promised the constant assistance of the Holy Spirit. Let us read again the well-known text, which is ever new and up-to-date. "All authority in Heaven and on earth has been given to me. Go therefore and make disciples of all nations, baptizing them in the name of the Father and of the Son and of the Holy Spirit, teaching them to observe all that I have commanded you; and behold, I am with you always, to the close of the age." [35]

12

The preaching of the gospel does not arise in Palestine through the personal initiative of a few fervent individuals. What could the Apostles do? They were nothing in their time. From a human point of view they were neither rich, nor learned, nor heroes. Jesus places on the shoulders of a handful of disciples an immense, divine task: "You did not choose me, but I chose you and appointed you that you should go and bear fruit and that your fruit should abide; so that whatever you ask the Father in my name, he may give it to you." [36]

Through two thousand years of history, the apostolic succession has been preserved in the Church. "The bishops," declares the Council of Trent, "have succeeded in the place of the Apostles and are placed, as the Apostle [Paul] himself says, by the Holy Spirit to rule the Church of God (Acts 20:28)." [37] And, among the Apostles, Christ himself made Simon the object of special attention. "You are Peter and on this rock I will build my church!" [38] "I have prayed for you that your faith may not fail; and when you have turned again, strengthen your brethren." [39]

Peter moves to Rome and there establishes the see of primacy of the Vicar of Christ. For this reason it is in Rome that the apostolic succession is seen most clearly. And for this reason Rome is called the apostolic see by antonomasia. The First Vatican Council proclaimed, with the words of a prior council, that of Florence: "All the faithful of Christ must believe that the Holy Apostolic See and the Roman Pontiff possess primacy over the whole world, and that the same Roman Pontiff is the successor of blessed Peter, prince of the Apostles, and true vicar of Jesus Christ, and head of all the Church, and father and teacher of all Christians; and that to him was given by our Lord Jesus Christ, in the person of blessed Peter, full power to feed, rule, and govern the universal Church." [40]

13   The supreme power of the Roman Pontiff and his infallibility, when he speaks *ex cathedra*, are not human inventions. They are based on the explicit foundational will of Christ. How foolish it is, then, to confront the government of the Pope with that of the bishops, or to reduce the validity of the pontifical Magisterium to the consent of the faithful! Nothing is more foreign to it than a balance of powers; human molds of thought do not help us, no matter how attractive or functional they may be. No one in the Church enjoys absolute power by himself, as man. In the Church there is no leader other than Christ. And Christ constituted a vicar of his—the Roman Pontiff—for his wayfaring spouse on earth.

The Church is apostolic by constitution. "That which truly is, and is called catholic, should stand out at one and the same time by the prerogatives of unity, holiness and apostolic succession. In that way, the Church is one, with a clear and perfect unity of the whole world and all nations, with that unity of which the principle, root, and indefectible origin is the supreme authority and most excellent primacy of blessed Peter, prince of the Apostles, and his successors in the Roman See. And there is no other Catholic Church, but that one which, built on the one Peter, rises up on the unity of the faith and on charity in one unique body, joined together and compact."[41]

We help to make that apostolic continuity more evident in the eyes of all men by demonstrating with exquisite fidelity our union with the Pope, which is union with Peter. Love for the Roman Pontiff must be in us a delightful passion, for in him we see Christ. If we deal with the Lord in prayer, we will go forward with a clear gaze that will permit us to perceive the action of the Holy Spirit, even in the face of events we do not understand or which produce sighs or sorrow.

The apostolic mission of all Catholics

The Church sanctifies us after we enter into her bosom   14
through Baptism. Newly born into natural life, we can already take refuge in sanctifying grace. "The faith of one person, even more, the faith of the whole Church, benefits the child through the action of the Holy Spirit, which gives unity to the Church and communicates the goods of one another." [42] This supernatural maternity of the Church, which the Holy Spirit confers, is truly marvelous. "Spiritual rebirth which is brought about by Baptism is in some way similar to bodily birth. Just as children in the womb of their mothers do not feed themselves, but rather are nourished from the sustenance of the mother, so also the little ones who do not have the use of reason and are like children in the womb of their mother the

Church, receive salvation through the action of the Church and not by themselves." [43]

The priestly power of the Church, which proceeds directly from Christ, stands out in all its greatness. "Christ is the source of every priesthood: for the priesthood of the Old Law was as its figure: but the priesthood of the New Law acts in the person of Christ, as is written in 2 Cor [2:10]: What I have forgiven, if I have forgiven anything, has been for your sake in the person of Christ." [44]

The saving mediation between God and man is perpetuated in the Church through the sacrament of Holy Orders, which gives to men the power—through sacramental character and consequent graces—to act as ministers of Jesus Christ on behalf of all souls. "That one person can carry out an act that another cannot does not stem from a difference of goodness or malice, but from an acquired power, which one possesses and the other does not. Therefore, since the layman does not receive the power to consecrate, he cannot bring about the consecration, no matter what his personal goodness may be." [45]

15   In the Church there is a diversity of ministries, but there is only one aim: the sanctification of men. And in this task all Christians participate in some way, through the character imprinted by the sacraments of Baptism and Confirmation. We must all feel responsible for the mission of the Church, which is the mission of Christ. He who does not have zeal for the salvation of souls, he who does not strive with all his strength to make the name and doctrine of Christ known and loved, will not understand the apostolicity of the Church.

A passive Christian has failed to understand what Christ wants from all of us. A Christian *who goes his own way*, unconcerned about the salvation of others, does not love with the heart of Jesus. Apostolate is not a mission reserved for the hierarchy, priests, and religious. The Lord calls all of us to be, with our example and word, instruments of the stream of grace which springs up to eternal life.

Whenever we read the Acts of the Apostles, we are moved by the audacity, the confidence in their mission, and the sacrificing joy of the disciples of Christ. They do not ask for multitudes. Even though the multitudes come, they address themselves to each particular soul, to each man, one by one. Philip, to the Ethiopian;[46] Peter, to the centurion;[47] Paul, to Sergius Paulus.[48]

They have learned from the Master. Remember the parable of the laborers who awaited work in the middle of the marketplace of the village? When the owner of the vineyard went out, already late in the day, he found that there were still laborers standing idle. "Why do you stand here idle all day?" he said to them. "Because no one has hired us," [49] they answered. This should not happen in the life of a Christian. No one should be found around him who can assert that he has not heard of Christ because no one has bothered to tell him.

Men often think that nothing prevents them from leaving God out of their lives. They deceive themselves. Though they may not know it, they are stretched out like the paralytic at the pool of Bethsaida—unable to move toward the waters which save, toward the doctrine which puts joy into the soul. So often the blame lies with Christians. The lame and sick of soul could repeat: *hominem non habeo*,[50] I do not have even one person to help me. Every Christian should be an apostle, because God, who does not need anyone, nevertheless needs us. He counts on us to dedicate ourselves to propagating his saving doctrine.

We are contemplating the mystery of the one, holy, catholic, and apostolic Church. It is time to ask ourselves: Do I share with Christ his zeal for souls? Do I pray for the Church of which I form part, in which I must carry out a specific mission that no one else can do for me? To be in the Church is

16

already much, but it is not enough. We must *be* the Church, because our Mother must never be a stranger to us, something external, foreign to our deepest thoughts.

Let us conclude our consideration of the marks of the Church. With the help of the Lord they will become engraved on our souls, and we will be confirmed by this clear, sure, divine criterion in order to love more this holy Mother who has brought us to the life of grace and who nourishes us, day by day, with inexhaustible care.

If by chance you hear offensive words or shouts hurled against the Church, show their loveless authors, with humanity and charity, that they cannot mistreat a mother in that way. They attack her now with impunity, because her kingdom, which is that of her Master and Founder, is not of this world. "As long as the wheat groans among the straw, as long as the spikes of wheat sigh among the cockle, as long as the vessels of mercy lament among those of ire, as long as the lily sobs among the thorns, there will always be enemies who say: when will she die and her name perish? They think: there will come a time in which the Church will disappear and there will be no more Christians. . . . But, when they say this, they of necessity die. And the Church remains."[51]

No matter what happens, Christ will not abandon his spouse. The Church triumphant is already with him at the right hand of the Father. And our Christian brothers beckon us to join them there, they who glorify God for this reality which we still see in the clear shadow of faith: the one, holy, catholic, and apostolic Church.

The Supernatural Aim of the Church

A homily given on May 28, 1972

Let me begin by reminding you of something Saint Cyprian tells us: "The universal Church is a people which derives its unity from the unity of the Father, of the Son and of the Holy Spirit." [1] It is not out of place therefore to preach about the Church on this feast of the most Blessed Trinity. The Church is rooted in this fundamental mystery of our catholic faith: the mystery of God, who is one in essence and three in persons.

The Fathers all see the Church as centered in the Trinity. Look how clearly Saint Augustine puts it: "God then dwells in his temple. Not only the Holy Spirit but also the Father and the Son. . . . Therefore, the holy Church is the temple of God, the temple of the entire Trinity." [2]

Next Sunday when we gather again, we will consider another marvelous aspect of the Church. We will fix our attention on the marks of the Church, which we will recite in a few moments in the Creed after singing our belief in the Father, in the Son, and in the Holy Spirit: *Et in Spiritum Sanctum*, we say, and *in unam, sanctam, catholicam et apostolicam Ecclesiam*.[3] We confess that there is only one Church which is holy, catholic, and apostolic.

All those who have truly loved the Church have known how to relate these four marks to the doctrine of the Blessed Trinity, which is the most ineffable mystery of our faith. "We believe in the one, holy, catholic, and apostolic Church of God, in which we receive the faith. In her we know the Father, Son, and Holy Spirit and are baptized in the name of the Father, and of the Son, and of the Holy Spirit." [4]

Difficult moments

18   We need to meditate frequently on the fact that the Church is a deep, great mystery, so that we never forget it. We cannot fully understand the Church on this earth. If men, using only their reason, were to analyze it, they would see only a group of people who abide by certain precepts and think in a similar way. But that would not be the Church.

In the Church we Catholics find our faith, our norms of conduct, our prayer, our sense of fraternity. Through it we are united with all our brothers who have already left this life and are being cleansed in Purgatory—the Church suffering—and with those who already enjoy the beatific vision and love forever the thrice holy God—the Church triumphant. The Church is in our midst and at the same time transcends history. It was born under the mantle of our Lady and continues to praise her on earth and in Heaven as its Mother.

Let us strengthen our faith in the supernatural character of the Church. Let us profess it with shouts, if necessary, for there are many, physically within the Church and even in high places, who have forgotten these capital truths. They try to propose an image of the Church which is neither holy nor one. Neither would it be apostolic, since it is not founded on the rock of Peter. Their substitute is not catholic, because it is riddled with unwarranted irregularities which are mere human caprices.

This is nothing new. Since Jesus Christ our Lord founded the Church, this Mother of ours has suffered constant persecution. In times past the attacks were delivered openly. Now, in many cases, persecution is disguised. But today, as yesterday, the Church continues to be buffeted from many sides.

Let me say once again that I am not a pessimist by habit or by temperament. How can we be pessimistic if our Lord has promised that he will be with us until the end of the world?[5]

The effusion of the Holy Spirit upon the Apostles gathered together in the Cenacle provided the first public manifestation of the Church.[6]

Our Father God is a loving Father. To help us understand this, Scripture graphically tells us that he takes care of us like "the apple of his eye."[7] He never ceases to sanctify, through the Holy Spirit, the Church founded by his beloved Son. But the Church is going through difficult moments. Confused shouting is heard on all sides, and all the errors that have occurred in the course of the centuries are reappearing with great fanfare.

Faith. We need faith. If we look with the eyes of faith, we   19 will see that the "Church carries within herself the explanation for her existence and purpose. Anyone who contemplates her with eyes filled with love for the truth must recognize that, quite independently of those who are her members and the ways in which the reality that is the Church is expressed in the material world, she carries within herself a unique and universal message of light, which is liberating, necessary and divine."[8]

We cannot help but feel sadness invade our soul when we hear heretical voices around us. And that is what they are, for I have never liked euphemisms. We see that the sanctity of marriage and of the priesthood is attacked without fear of rebuke. We see people deny the Immaculate Conception and the perpetual virginity of our holy Mother Mary, along with all the other privileges and gifts with which God adorned her. We see the perpetual miracle of the Real Presence of Jesus Christ in the Holy Eucharist, the primacy of Peter, and even the Resurrection of our Lord put in doubt. How can anyone not feel tempted to sadness? Have confidence, for the Church is incorruptible. "The Church will shake if her foundation shifts; but can Christ be moved? As long as Christ remains her immovable base, the Church will remain strong until the end of time."[9]

Human and divine elements in the Church

20   Just as in Christ there are two natures, both a human and a divine one, so by analogy we can refer to the presence in the Church of human and divine elements. No one can fail to see the human part. The Church, in this world, is for men, who are its raw material. And when we speak of men we speak of freedom, which permits the coexistence of grandeur and meanness, of heroism and failure.

If we were to focus only on the human side of the Church, we would never understand her. We would still be distant from the threshold of her central mystery. Sacred Scripture uses many terms derived from everyday life to describe God's kingdom and its presence among us in the Church. It compares her to a sheepfold, to a flock, to a house, to a seed, to a vine, to a field in which God plants or builds. But one expression stands out and sums up all the rest: the Church is Christ's body.

"And his gifts were that some should be apostles, some prophets, some evangelists, some pastors and teachers, for the equipment of the saints, for the work of ministry, for building up the body of Christ." [10] Saint Paul also writes that all of us, "though many, are one body in Christ, and individually members of one another." [11] How luminous is our faith! We are all in Christ, for "He is the head of the body, the Church." [12]

21   This is the faith which Christians have always professed. Listen with me to what Saint Augustine tells us: "The whole Christ is made up of head and body, a truth which I am sure you know well. The head is our Savior himself, who suffered under Pontius Pilate, and now, after his resurrection from among the dead, is seated at the right hand of the Father. And his body is the Church. Not this or that church but the Church that is spread throughout the world. Not only the one which

exists among the men now living, for those who went before us and those who are to come to the end of the world also belong to it. The entire Church, formed by the assembly of all the faithful since all of them are members of Christ, has Christ as its head. He governs his body from Heaven. And although the head is not visible to the body, it is united to it by love." [13]

You should understand now why the visible Church cannot be severed from the invisible. The Church is, at one and the same time, a mystical body and a juridical body. Pope Leo XIII tells us: "By the very fact that it is a body, the Church is visible to the eyes." [14] In the visible body of the Church, in the behavior of men who make it up here on earth, we find weaknesses, vacillations, and acts of treason. But that is not the whole Church, nor is it to be confused with this unworthy behavior. On the other hand, here and now, there is no shortage of generosity, of heroism, of holy lives that make no noise, that are spent with joy in the service of their brothers in the faith and of all souls.

I would also like you to consider that even if human failings were to outnumber acts of valor, the clear undeniable mystical reality of the Church, though unperceived by the senses, would still remain. The Church would still be the Body of Christ, our Lord himself, the action of the Holy Spirit and the loving presence of the Father.

The Church is, therefore, inseparably human and divine. "It is a divine society in origin, and supernatural in its aim and in the means that are directly ordered to this end. But in so far as it is made up of men, it is a human community." [15] It lives and acts in the world, but its goal and strength are not here but in Heaven.

It would be a serious mistake to attempt to separate the *charismatic* Church, supposedly the sole follower of Christ's spirit, from the juridical or *institutional* Church, the handiwork of men, subject to historical vicissitudes. There is only one Church. Christ founded only one Church, which is visible and invisible. It has a hierarchical and organized body and a fundamental structure by divine law, with an intimate supernatural life that animates, sustains, and vivifies it.

We cannot fail to recall that when Christ instituted his Church, "he did not conceive it or form it in such a way that it would contain a number of generically similar but distinct communities without the bonds that make the Church indivisible and singular. . . . And thus when Jesus spoke of this mystical edifice, he mentions only one Church which he calls his own: 'I will build my Church' (Mt 16:18). Any other one you can imagine outside of this cannot be his true Church since it was not founded by him." [16]

Faith, I repeat. Let us believe more, asking the Blessed Trinity, whose feast we celebrate today, for greater faith. Anything can happen, except for the thrice holy God to abandon his spouse.

The Church's aim

23   In the first chapter of his letter to the Ephesians, Saint Paul affirms that the mystery of God, announced by Christ, is carried out in the Church. God the Father "has put all things under his feet and has made him the head over all things for the church, which is his body, the fullness of him who fills all in all." [17] "The mystery of God is to set forth in Christ as a plan for the fullness of time, to unite all things in him, things in Heaven and things on earth." [18]

"It is an inscrutable mystery, of pure gratuitous love. For he chose us in him before the foundation of the world, that we should be holy and blameless before him." [19] God's love is limitless. Saint Paul also tells us that our Savior "desires all men to be saved and to come to the knowledge of the truth." [20]

This, and no other, is the aim of the Church: the salvation of souls, one by one. For this reason the Father sent his Son, "and now I am sending you out in my turn." [21] This is the origin of the command to teach his doctrine and to baptize, so that the most Blessed Trinity may live in men's souls in grace. "All authority in Heaven and on earth has been given to me. Go therefore and make disciples of all nations, baptizing them in the name of the Father and of the Son and of the Holy Spirit, teaching them to observe all that I have commanded you; and behold, I am with you always, to the close of the age." [22]

In those simple and sublime words that conclude Saint Matthew's gospel we find the obligation to preach the truths of faith, the need for sacramental life, the promise of Christ's continual assistance to his Church. You cannot be faithful to our Lord if you neglect these supernatural demands: to instruct in Christian faith and morality and to frequent the sacraments. It is with this mandate that Christ founded his Church. Everything else is secondary.

Salvation in the Church

We cannot forget that the Church is not merely a way of salvation; it is the only way. This is not a human opinion, but the express will of Christ: "He who believes and is baptized will be saved; but he who does not believe will be condemned." [23] This is why we assert that the Church is a necessary means of salvation. No later than the second century, Origen wrote: "If anyone wants to be saved, let him come to this house so that he can obtain salvation. . . . Let no one deceive himself: outside of this house, that is, outside of the Church, no one will be saved." [24] Of the deluge, Saint Cyprian says: "If someone had escaped outside of Noah's ark then we would admit that someone who abandoned the Church might escape condemnation." [25]

Extra Ecclesiam, nulla salus. That is the continual warning of the Fathers. "Outside the Catholic Church you can find everything except salvation," Saint Augustine admits. "You can have honor and sacraments: you can sing 'alleluia' and respond 'amen.' You can uphold the gospel, have faith in the Father, in the Son, and in the Holy Spirit, and preach that faith. But never, except in the catholic Church, can you find salvation." [26]

Nonetheless, as Pius XII lamented little more than twenty years ago, "some reduce to an empty formula the need to pertain to the true Church in order to obtain eternal salvation." [27] This dogma of faith is at the root of the Church's coredemptive activity. It spells out the Christian's grave apostolic responsibility. Among Christ's express commandments is the categorical one to incorporate ourselves in his Mystical Body by Baptism. "And our Savior not only commanded that everyone enter the Church, but also established that the Church be the means of salvation, without which no one can reach the kingdom of celestial glory." [28]

It is a matter of faith that anyone who does not belong to the Church will not be saved; and anyone who is not baptized does not enter the Church. Justification "cannot take place after the promulgation of the gospel, without Baptism or its desire," the Council of Trent established. [29]

25   This is a continual demand of the Church which on the one hand stimulates us to greater apostolic zeal, and on the other manifests clearly the infinite mercy of God with his creatures.

This is how Saint Thomas explained it: "The sacrament of Baptism may be wanting to someone in two ways. First, in reality and desire, as is the case of those who are neither baptized nor wish to be baptized: which clearly indicates contempt of the sacrament for those who have the use of reason. Consequently, those to whom Baptism is wanting thus cannot obtain salvation: since neither sacramentally nor spiritually are they incorporated in Christ, through whom alone can salvation be obtained. Secondly, the sacrament of Baptism may be wanting to someone in reality but not in desire: for instance, when a man wishes to be baptized, but by some misfortune he is forestalled by death before receiving Baptism. Such a man can obtain salvation without actually being baptized, on account of desire for Baptism, a desire which is the outcome of faith that works by charity, whereby God, whose power is not tied to visible sacraments, sanctifies man inwardly." [30]

God our Lord denies no one supernatural and eternal happiness, although it is a completely free gift to which no one has a right, especially after sin. His generosity is infinite. "It is a matter of common knowledge that those who suffer invincible ignorance of our most holy religion but carefully observe all the precepts of the Natural Law which are engraved by God in the hearts of all men, and want to obey God and lead an upright life, can obtain eternal life through the efficacious action of divine light and grace." [31]

God alone knows what goes on in the heart of each man, and he does not deal with souls *en masse*, but one by one. No one on this earth can make a judgment about the eternal salvation or condemnation of any individual.

Let us not forget that conscience can be culpably deformed and harden itself in sin, resisting the saving action of God. That is why it is necessary to spread Christ's doctrine, the truths of faith, and the norms of Christian morality. That is also why we need the sacraments, all of which were instituted by Jesus Christ as instrumental causes of his grace[32] and remedies for the weaknesses that ensue from our fallen nature.[33] Finally, that is why we need to receive frequently the sacraments of Penance and the Eucharist.

The awesome responsibility of all the Church's members

26

and especially of its shepherds is made clear in Saint Paul's advice: "I charge you in the presence of God and of Christ Jesus, who is to judge the living and the dead, and in the name of his coming and of his kingdom: Preach the word, be urgent in season and out of season, convince, rebuke, and exhort, be unfailing in patience and in teaching. For the time is coming when people will not endure sound teaching, but having itching ears they will accumulate for themselves teachers to suit their own likings, and will turn away from listening to the truth and wander into myths." [34]

A time of trial

27   I cannot say how often the prophetic words of the Apostle have been fulfilled, but you would have to be blind not to see how they are being carried out almost to the letter in our own time. People reject the doctrine contained in the law of God and of the Church. They twist the content of the beatitudes, translating them into a socio-political doctrine. They attack those who try to be humble, meek, and pure of heart as ignorant or outdated partisans of things long ago consigned to the past. They refuse to bear the yoke of chastity and invent a thousand excuses to evade Christ's divine precepts.

There is one symptom that sums up this whole situation: the attempt to change the supernatural aims of the Church. When they speak of *justice*, some people no longer understand by it a life of sanctity, but a particular political struggle, more or less influenced by Marxism, which is incompatible with the Christian faith. For them, *liberation* does not imply a personal battle to flee from sin, but merely a human task that may be noble and just in itself but that is meaningless for a Christian, if it implies losing sight of the one thing necessary[35]—the eternal salvation of souls, one by one.

With a blindness that comes from separating themselves   28
from God—"this people honors me with their lips, but their
heart is far from me"[36]—some fabricate an image of the
Church that has nothing to do with what Christ founded.
Even the holy sacrament of the altar, the renewal of the
sacrifice of Calvary, is profaned or reduced to a mere symbol
of what they call the "communion of men with each other."
What would have become of souls if our Lord had not sacrificed himself for us, to the last drop of his precious Blood?
How can they despise this perpetual miracle of the Real Presence of Christ in the tabernacle? He has stayed with us so that
we can talk to him and adore him. He has stayed with us as a
foretaste of our future glory, so that we decide once and for
all to follow in his footsteps.

These are times of trial, and we have to ask the Lord with
an unceasing clamor[37] to shorten them, to look mercifully on
his Church, and to grant once again his supernatural light to
the souls of her shepherds and of all the faithful. The Church
has no reason to try to pander to men, since they, individually
or in community, cannot save themselves. The only one who
saves is God.

Loving the Church

We need to shout out loudly today—time and again—those   29
bold words of Saint Peter to a group of important people in
Jerusalem: "This is the stone which was rejected by you
builders, but which has become the head of the corner. And
there is salvation in no one else, for there is no other name
under Heaven given among men by which we must be
saved."[38]

Thus spoke the first Pope, the rock on which Christ built
his Church. He was moved to do so by his filial devotion to
the Lord and by his solicitude for the little flock entrusted to

him. From him and from the rest of the Apostles, the first Christians learned to love the Church tenderly.

Have you seen, in contrast, how people talk heartlessly about our Holy Mother the Church nowadays? What a great consolation it is to read the ancient Fathers' ardent and loving phrases about the Church! "Let us love the Lord our God; let us love his Church," Saint Augustine writes. "Let us love Him as our Father, and her as our Mother. Let no one say: 'It is true that I still go to the idols and consult the possessed and the sorcerers, but I have not abandoned the Church, I am a Catholic.' You may still be united to your Mother, but you offend your Father. Someone else might say: 'God forbid. I do not consult sorcerers or the possessed. I do not practice sacrilegious prophecies nor go to adore demons nor serve gods of stone. But I belong to the Donatist party.' What use will it be to him not to offend his Father if his Father will avenge his Mother whom he offends?"[39] And Saint Cyprian puts it more briefly: "No one can have God as his Father who does not have the Church as his Mother."[40]

In our days many refuse to listen to the true doctrine about our Mother the Church. Some want to *redesign* the institution, trying to introduce foolishly into the mystical body of Christ a democracy modeled on that of some civil societies. Or worse yet, they clamor for an ecclesiastical body whose members would be equal in every respect. They refuse to believe that by divine institution the Church is made up of the Pope with the bishops, priests, deacons, and lay people. That is how Christ wanted it to be.

30   The Church is by divine will a hierarchical institution. The Second Vatican Council describes it as a "society structured with hierarchical organs"[41] in which "the ministers are invested with a sacred power."[42] The hierarchy is not only compatible with freedom; it is at the service of the freedom of the children of God.[43]

The term *democracy* is meaningless in the Church which, let me insist, is hierarchical by divine will. But *hierarchy* means holy government and sacred order. In no way does it imply a merely human arbitrary order or a subhuman despotism. Our Lord established in the Church a hierarchical order that should not degenerate into tyranny, because authority is as much a call to serve as is obedience.

In the Church there is equality, because once baptized we are all equal, all children of the same God, our Father. There is no difference as Christians between the Pope and someone who has just joined the Church. But this radical equality does not mean that we can change the constitution of the Church in those things that were established by Christ. By expressed divine will there are different functions, which imply different capacities, an indelible *character* conferred on the sacred ministers by the sacrament of Orders. At the summit of this order is Peter's successor and, with him, and under him, all the bishops, with the triple mission of sanctifying, governing, and teaching.

Forgive me for being so insistent, but I must remind you again that the truths of the faith are not determined by majority vote. They make up the *depositum fidei*: the body of truths left by Christ to all of the faithful and entrusted to the Magisterium of the Church to be authentically taught and set forth.   31

It would be an error to think that since men seem to have become more aware of the bonds of mutual solidarity that unite them, we ought to change the constitution of the Church as if it needed updating. The times do not belong to men, whether ecclesiastics or not. The times are God's, who is the Lord of history. And the Church can bring salvation to souls only if she remains faithful to Christ in her constitution and teaching, both dogmatic and moral.

Let us reject, therefore, the suggestion that the Church,

ignoring the Sermon on the Mount, seeks a purely human happiness on earth, since we know that her only task is to bring men to eternal glory in Heaven. Let us reject any purely naturalistic view that fails to value the supernatural role of divine grace. Let us reject materialistic opinions that exclude spiritual values from human life. Let us equally reject any secularizing theory that aims to equate the aims of the Church with those of earthly states, distorting its essence, institutions, and activities into something similar to those of temporal society.

The depths of God's wisdom

32   Remember what Saint Paul told us in the epistle we read today: "O the depth of the riches and wisdom and knowledge of God! How unsearchable are his judgments and how inscrutable his ways! 'For who has known the mind of the Lord, or who has been his counselor? Or who has given a gift to him that he might be repaid?' For from him and through him and to him are all things. To him be glory forever. Amen." [44] In the light of God's words, how petty seem human designs when they are used to undermine what our Lord has established!

But I do not want you to ignore the fact that on all sides we find evidence of man's warped behavior. Not being able to get around God, he turns and takes revenge on other men. Contemporaries of ours become terrible instruments of evil when they serve as occasion and inducement to sin, sowing confusion, which leads people to commit intrinsically evil actions and flaunt them as good.

There has always been ignorance. But nowadays the most abysmal ignorance in matters of faith and morals is disguised at times with high-sounding terms that appear theological. That is why Christ's commandment to his Apostles that we have just heard in the Gospel, "Go and teach all nations," [45] takes on, if possible, an even more pressing urgency. We cannot be indifferent. We cannot fold our arms and go into seclusion within ourselves. Let us step forward to fight, for God, a great battle of peace, serenity, and doctrine.

We must be understanding, covering everything over with   33
the kind mantle of charity. But charity must strengthen us in the faith, increase our hope, and make us strong to say loud and clear that the Church is not what some people pretend. The Church belongs to God and has only one aim, the salvation of souls. Let us draw near to our Lord and speak to him face to face in our prayer. Let us ask him forgiveness for our personal weaknesses, and let us make reparation for our sins and for those of other men who may not realize in this climate of confusion how gravely they are offending God.

In the Holy Mass this Sunday, in the unbloody renewal of the sacrifice of Calvary, Jesus Christ, Priest and Victim, will offer himself for the sins of men. Let us not leave him alone. Let there well up in our heart an ardent desire to be with him, next to the Cross. May our clamor rise to the Father, the merciful God, asking him to give back peace to the world, peace to the Church, peace to consciences.

If we do this, we will find next to the Cross Mary Most Holy, the Mother of God and our Mother. And guided by her blessed hand, we will come to Jesus, and through him to the Father and the Holy Spirit.

A Priest Forever

A homily given on April 13, 1973

34 When saying Mass a few days ago I paused to reflect on a phrase from the psalms in the Communion Antiphon: "The Lord is my shepherd, I shall not want." [1] It reminded me of another psalm, which was used in the rite of tonsure: "The Lord is my chosen portion and my cup." [2] Christ Himself is placed in the hands of priests who thus become "the stewards of the mysteries"—of the wonders—"of God." [3]

Next summer some fifty members of Opus Dei will receive Holy Orders. Since 1944 small groups of members of the Work have been ordained, each ordination giving witness to the working of God's grace and to service to the Church. And yet each year some people are surprised. How is it, they ask, that thirty, forty, or fifty men whose lives are so rich in achievement and so full of promise are ready to become priests? I should like today to dwell on this subject—though I run the risk of adding to people's bewilderment.

Why be a priest?

35 The sacrament of Holy Orders is going to be conferred on this group of members of the Work who have had very substantial experience, perhaps over many years, in medicine, law, engineering, architecture, and many other professional activities. They are men whose work would allow them to aspire to more or less prominent positions m society.

They are being ordained to serve. They are not being ordained to give orders or to attract attention, but rather to give themselves to the service of all souls in a divine and continuous silence. When they become priests, they will not allow themselves to yield to the temptation to imitate the occupations of lay people—even though they are well able to do that work because they have been at it until now, and have acquired a lay outlook that they will never lose.

Their competence in the various branches of human knowledge, such as history, natural sciences, psychology, law, and sociology, is a necessary feature of this lay outlook. But it will not lead them to put themselves forward as priest-psychologists, priest-biologists, or priest-sociologists: they receive the sacrament of Holy Orders to become nothing other than *priest-priests*, priests through and through.

They probably know more about a wide range of secular, 36 human matters than many lay people. But the moment they are ordained they cheerfully silence this competence and concentrate on fortifying themselves through continuous prayer so as to speak only of God, to preach the gospel, and to administer the sacraments. If I can put it this way, I would say that this is their new professional work. To it they will devote their whole day and find that they still have not enough time to do all that has to be done. They have constantly to study theology; they must give spiritual guidance to very many souls, hear many confessions, preach tirelessly, and pray a great deal; their heart must always be focused on the tabernacle, where He who has chosen us to be His own is really present. Their life is a wonderful self-surrender, full of joy, though like everyone they will meet up with difficulties.

As I said, all this may serve to increase people's surprise. Perhaps some may still ask themselves: What is the point of this renunciation of so many good and noble things of the earth? These men could have had a successful professional career. Through their example they could have exerted a Christian influence on society, on cultural, educational, financial, and many other aspects of civil life.

Others will remind you that in many places today the idea of the priesthood is very confused. They keep on saying that you must search for the *identity* of the priest, and they question the value of giving oneself to God in the priesthood in present-day society. And then others will ask how it is that, at a time when vocations to the priesthood are in short supply, this very vocation should arise among Christians who, thanks to their own efforts, have already found their place in society.

Priests and lay people

37   I can understand this surprise, but it would be insincere of me to say that I share it. These men become priests of their own free will, because they want to, and this is a very supernatural reason. They know that they are not renouncing anything in the normal sense of the word. Through their vocation to Opus Dei they have been devoted to the service of the Church and of all souls. This full, divine vocation led them to sanctify their work, to sanctify themselves in their work, and to seek the sanctification of others in the context of their professional relationships.

The members of Opus Dei, whether priests or lay people, are ordinary Christians, and, like all Christians, they are addressed by Saint Peter in these words: "You are a chosen race, a royal priesthood, a holy nation, God's own people, that you may declare the wonderful deeds of him who has called you out of darkness into his marvelous light. Once you were no people but now you are God's people; once you had not received mercy but now you have received mercy." [4]

As Christian faithful, priests and lay people share one and the same condition, for God our Lord has called us to the fullness of charity which is holiness: "Blessed be the God and Father of our Lord Jesus Christ who has blessed us in Christ with every spiritual blessing in the heavenly places, even as he chose us in him before the foundation of the world, that we should be holy and blameless before him." [5]

There is no such thing as second-class holiness. Either we put up a constant fight to stay in the grace of God and imitate Christ, our model, or we desert in that divine battle. God invites everyone; each person can become holy in his own state in life. In Opus Dei this passion for holiness, in spite of individual errors and failings, does not vary from priests to lay people; and besides, priests make up a very small part compared with the total number of members.

So if you look at things with the eyes of faith, there is no question of renunciation on entering the priesthood; nor does the priesthood imply a sort of summit of vocation to Opus Dei. Holiness does not depend on your state in life (married or single, widowed or ordained), but on the way you personally respond to the grace you receive. This grace teaches us to put away the works of darkness and put on the armor of light: which is serenity, peace, and joyful service, full of sacrifice to all mankind. [6]

The dignity of the priesthood

The priesthood leads one to serve God in a state that, in itself, is no better or worse than any other: it is simply different. But the priestly vocation is invested with a dignity and greatness that has no equal on earth. Saint Catherine of Siena put these words on Jesus' lips: "I do not wish the respect which priests should be given to be in any way diminished; for the reverence and respect which is shown them is not referred to them but to Me, by virtue of the Blood which I have given to them to administer. Were it not for this, you should render them the same reverence as lay people, and no more. . . . You must not offend them; by offending them you offend Me and

38

not them. Therefore I forbid it and I have laid it down that you shall not touch my Christs." [6]

Some people keep searching for what they call the identity of the priest. How clearly Saint Catherine expresses it! What is the identity of the priest? That of Christ. All of us Christians can and should be not just other Christs, *alter Christus*, but Christ himself: *ipse Christus!* But in the priest this happens in a direct way, by virtue of the sacrament.

39   "To accomplish so great a work"—the work of redemption—"Christ is always present in his Church, especially in her liturgical celebrations. He is present in the Sacrifice of the Mass, not only in the person of his minister, 'the same now offering through the ministry of priests, who formerly offered himself on the Cross,' but especially under the eucharistic species." [8] The sacrament of Orders, in effect, equips the priest to lend our Lord his voice, his hands, his whole being. It is Jesus Christ who, in the Holy Mass, through the words of the Consecration, changes the substance of the bread and wine into his Body, Soul, Blood, and Divinity.

This is the source of the priest's incomparable dignity. It is a greatness which is on loan: it is completely compatible with my own littleness. I pray to God our Lord to give all of us priests the grace to perform holy things in a holy way, to reflect in every aspect of our lives the wonders of the greatness of God. "Those of us who celebrate the mysteries of the Passion of our Lord must imitate what we perform. And then the host will take our place before God because we render ourselves hosts." [9]

If you ever come across a priest who apparently does not seem to be following the teaching of the gospel—do not judge him, let God judge him—bear in mind that if he celebrates Mass validly, with the intention of consecrating, our Lord will still come down into his hands, however unworthy they are. Where could you find greater self-surrender and annihilation? Here it is greater than in Bethlehem or on Calvary. Why? Because Jesus' heart, filled with a desire to redeem, does not want anyone to be able to say that he has not been called. He goes out to meet those who do not seek Him.

That is Love! There is no other explanation for it. When it comes to speaking of Christ's love, we are lost for words. He has so abased Himself that he accepts everything; he exposes himself to everything—to sacrilege, to blasphemy, and to the cold indifference of so many people—in order to offer even one man the chance of hearing the beating of his heart in his wounded side.

Here we have the priest's identity: he is a direct and daily instrument of the saving grace that Christ has won for us. If you grasp this, if you meditate on it in the active silence of prayer, how could you ever think of the priesthood in terms of renunciation? It is a gain, an incalculable gain. Our Mother Mary, the holiest of creatures—only God is holier—brought Jesus Christ into the world just once; priests bring him on earth, to our soul and body, every day: Christ comes to be our food, to give us life, to be, even now, a pledge of future life.

The common priesthood and the ministerial priesthood

A priest is no more a man or a Christian than any ordinary lay   40
person. That is why it is so important for a priest to be deeply humble. He must understand that these words of Saint Paul also apply to him in a special way: "What have you that you did not receive?" [10] What he has received . . . is God! He has received the power to celebrate the Holy Eucharist, the Holy Mass (the principal purpose of priestly ordination), to forgive sins, to administer the other sacraments, and to preach with authority the Word of God, governing the rest of

the faithful in those matters which refer to the kingdom of Heaven.

41   "While it indeed presupposes the sacraments of Christian initiation, the priesthood of priests is nevertheless conferred by its own special sacrament. Through that sacrament priests, by the anointing of the Holy Spirit, are marked with a special character and are so configured to Christ the Priest that they can act in the person of Christ the Head." [11] That is the way the Church is. It does not depend on man's whim but on the express will of Jesus Christ its founder. "Sacrifice and priesthood are so united by God's ordination, that in both laws"—the old and the new covenant—"both have existed. Since therefore the Catholic Church in the New Testament has received, through the Lord's institution, the visible sacrifice of the Eucharist, we must also hold that she has a new priesthood, visible and external, which has taken the place of the old priesthood." [12]

In those who have been ordained, the ministerial priesthood is added to the common priesthood of all of the faithful. Therefore, although it would be a serious error to argue that a priest is more a member of the faithful than an unordained Christian is, it can, on the other hand, be said that he is more a priest: like all Christians he belongs to the priestly people redeemed by Christ, and in addition to this he is marked with a character of the priestly ministry which differentiates him *essentially and not only in degree*[13] from the common priesthood of the faithful.

42   I cannot understand why some priests are so eager to be indistinguishable from other Christians, forgetting or neglecting their specific mission in the Church, that for which they have been ordained. They seem to think that Christians want to see the priest as just another man. That is not so. They want to find in the priest those virtues proper to every Christian and, indeed, every honorable man: understanding, jus-

tice, a life of work—priestly work, in this instance—and good manners.

But the faithful also want to be able to recognize clearly the priestly character: they expect the priest to pray, not to refuse to administer the sacraments; they expect him to be open to everyone and not set himself up to take charge of people or become an aggressive leader of human factions, of whatever shade.[14] They expect him to bring love and devotion to the celebration of the Holy Mass, to sit in the confessional, to console the sick and the troubled; to teach sound doctrine to children and adults, to preach the Word of God and no mere human science which—no matter how well he may know it—is not the knowledge that saves and brings eternal life; they expect him to give counsel and be charitable to those in need.

In a word: they ask the priest to learn how not to hamper   43 the presence of Christ in him, especially in those moments when he is offering the Sacrifice of the Body and Blood and when, in God's name, he forgives sins in secret, private, sacramental confession. The administration of these two sacraments has so important a part in the priest's mission that everything should hinge on it. Other priestly tasks, such as preaching and giving instruction in the faith, would lack solid foundation if they were not aimed at teaching people to relate to Christ, to meet him in the loving tribunal of Penance and in the unbloody renewal of the Sacrifice of Calvary, the Mass.

Let me dwell just a little longer on the Holy Sacrifice: for if the Mass is, for us, the center and root of our lives as Christians, it must be so in a special way in the priest's life. A priest who, for no good reason, does not celebrate the Holy Sacrifice of the altar every day,[15] would show little love of God. It would be as though he wanted to reproach Christ by stating that he did not share Christ's desire for redemption, that he did not understand his impatience to give himself, defenseless, as food for the soul.

A priest to say Mass

44   We must remember that all of us priests, saints or sinners, are not ourselves when we celebrate Holy Mass. We are Christ, who renews on the altar his divine sacrifice of Calvary. "In the mystery of the eucharistic sacrifice, in which priests fulfil their principal function, the work of our redemption is continually carried out. For this reason its daily celebration is earnestly recommended. This celebration is an act of Christ and the Church even if it is impossible for the faithful to be present." [16]

The Council of Trent teaches that "in the Mass is performed, contained and sacrificed, in an unbloody manner, that same Christ who once and for all offered Himself in a bloody manner on the altar of the Cross . . . thus the Victim is one and the same; and he who is now offered through the ministry of priests is the same as he who offered himself on the Cross; only the manner of offering is different." [17]

The fact that the faithful attend or do not attend Holy Mass in no way changes this truth of faith. When I celebrate Mass surrounded by people I am very happy; I don't need to think of myself as president of any kind of assembly. I am, on the one hand, a member of the faithful like the others; but, above all, I am Christ at the Altar! I am renewing in an unbloody manner the divine Sacrifice of Calvary and I am consecrating, *in persona Christi*, in the person of Christ. I really represent Jesus Christ, for I am lending him my body, my voice, my hands, and my poor heart, so often stained, which I want him to purify.

When I celebrate Mass with just one person to serve it, the people are present also. I feel that there, with me, are all

Catholics, all believers, and also all those who do not believe. All God's creatures are there—the earth and the sea and the sky, and the animals and plants—the whole of creation giving glory to the Lord.

And especially I will say, using the words of the Second 45 Vatican Council, that "we are most closely united to the worshipping church in Heaven as we join with and venerate first of all the memory of the glorious ever Virgin Mary, of Saint Joseph and the blessed Apostles and martyrs, and of all the saints." [18]

I ask all Christians to pray earnestly for us priests that we learn to perform the Holy Sacrifice in a holy way. I ask you to show a deep love for the Holy Mass and in this way to encourage us priests to celebrate it respectfully, with divine and human dignity: looking after the cleanliness of the vestments and other things used for worship, devoutly, without rushing.

Why the hurry? Do people in love hurry when they are saying goodbye? They seem to be going and then they don't go; they turn back once and again; they repeat quite ordinary words as if they had just discovered their meaning . . . please don't take exception to my applying to the things of God the example of noble and fine human love. If we love God with our heart of flesh—and we have no other—we will not be in a hurry to finish this meeting, this loving appointment with Him.

Some priests take it all very coolly. They don't mind stringing out the readings, announcements, and notices until we are tired of them. But when the main part of the Mass arrives, the Sacrifice proper, they actually rush. This means that the rest of the faithful do not devoutly adore Christ, Priest and Victim; nor do they learn to thank him, calmly and respectfully, after Mass for his having come among us once again.

In the Holy Mass, all the affections and needs of a Christian's heart find their best channel: through Christ the Mass leads to the Father in the Holy Spirit. The priest should make a special effort to ensure that people know this and put it into practice. No other activity should, normally, take precedence over this task of teaching people to love and venerate the Holy Eucharist.

46   "The priest carries out two acts: the principal one is an action on the true Body of Christ; the secondary one affects the Mystical Body of Christ. The second act or ministry depends on the first, but the reverse is not the case." [19]

Therefore the most important part of the priestly ministry consists in trying to get Catholics to approach the Holy Sacrifice with growing purity, humility, and devotion. If a priest strives to do this, he will not be cheated, nor will he defraud the consciences of his fellow Christians.

In the Holy Mass what we do is adore: we fulfill lovingly the first duty of a creature to his Creator: You "shall worship the Lord your God and Him only shall you serve." [20] Not the cold, external adoration of a servant, but an intimate esteem and attachment that befits the tender love of a son.

In the Holy Mass we find the perfect opportunity to atone for our sins and the sins of all men, so as to be able to say with Saint Paul that we are completing in our flesh what is lacking in the sufferings of Christ. [21] No one is an isolated individual in this world; no one can consider himself completely free from blame for the evil that is done on earth, which is the result of original sin and the sum total of many personal sins. Let us love sacrifice; let us seek atonement. How? By uniting ourselves in the Mass to Christ, who is Priest and Victim. He is always the one who bears the tremendous weight of the infidelities of men—your infidelities and mine.

47   The Sacrifice of Calvary is an infinite expression of Christ's generosity. It is true that each of us is very much out for himself; but God our Lord does not mind if we lay all our needs before him at Mass. Who doesn't have things to ask for?

Lord, this illness . . . Lord, this sorrow . . . Lord, that humiliation which I don't seem to be able to bear out of love for You. . . . We desire the welfare, joy, and happiness of the people in our own home; we are saddened by the condition of those who hunger and thirst for bread and for justice, of those who experience the bitterness of loneliness and of those who end their days without an affectionate smile or a helping hand.

But what really makes us suffer, the greatest human failure we want to remedy, is sin, separation from God, the danger that souls may be lost for all eternity. Our overriding desire when we celebrate Mass is the same as Christ's when he offered himself on Calvary: to bring men to eternal glory in the love of God.

Let us get used to speaking sincerely to our Lord when he comes down to the altar, an innocent Victim in the hands of the priest. Confidence in the help of God will give us a sensitivity of soul which is expressed in good works: charity, understanding, tender sympathy for those who suffer and for those who pretend to be happy enjoying false and empty joys, which soon turn to sadness.

Finally, we give thanks to God our Lord for the wonderful way he has given himself up for us. Imagine, the Word made flesh has come to us as our food! . . . Inside us, inside our littleness, lies the Creator of Heaven and earth! . . . The Virgin Mary was conceived without sin to prepare her to receive Christ in her womb. If our thanksgiving were in proportion to the difference between the gift and our desserts, should we not turn the whole day into a continuous Eucharist, a continuous thanksgiving? Do not leave the church almost immediately after receiving the Sacrament. Surely you have nothing so important on that you cannot give our Lord ten minutes to say *thanks*. Let's not be mean. Love is repaid with love.

A priest forever

49   A priest who says the Mass in this way—adoring, atoning, pleading, giving thanks, identifying himself with Christ—and who teaches others to make the Sacrifice of the altar the center and root of the Christian life really will show the incomparable value of his vocation, the value of that character with which he has been stamped and which he will never lose.

I know that you will understand what I mean when I say that, compared with a priest like that, those who behave as if they wanted to apologize for being ministers of God are nothing less than a failure—a human and Christian failure. It is most unfortunate because it leads them to give up the ministry, to ape lay people, and to look for a second job, which gradually takes over from the task that is proper to their vocation and their mission. Often when they flee from giving spiritual attention to souls, they tend to replace this with another occupation (moving into those areas which belong to lay people—social action and politics), and we get the phenomenon of *clericalism*, the true priestly mission gone wrong.

50   I do not wish to conclude on a somber note that might sound pessimistic. The genuine Christian priesthood has not disappeared from God's Church. The teaching which we have received from the divine lips of Jesus has not changed. There are many thousands of priests throughout the world who really do respond to their vocation, quietly, undramatically. They have not fallen into the temptation to throw overboard a treasure of holiness and grace that has existed in the Church from the very beginning.

It warms my heart to think of the quiet human and supernatural dignity of those brothers of mine, scattered throughout the world. It is only right that they should now feel themselves surrounded by the friendship, help, and affection of many Christians. And when the moment comes for them to enter God's presence, Jesus will go out to meet them. He will glorify forever those who have acted on earth in his Person and in his name. He will shower them with that grace of which they have been ministers.

Let us return again to those members of Opus Dei who are being ordained next summer. Do please pray for them, so that they will always be faithful, devout, learned, committed, and happy priests. Commend them especially to our Lady. Ask her to take special care of those who will spend their lives serving her Son, our Lord Jesus Christ, the eternal Priest.

Passionately Loving the World

A homily given on October 8, 1967

51   You have just been listening to the solemn reading of the two
texts of Sacred Scripture for the Mass of the twenty-first Sunday after Pentecost. Having heard the Word of God you are
already in the right atmosphere for the words I want to address to you: words of a priest, spoken to a large family of the
children of God in his Holy Church. Words, therefore, which
are intended to be supernatural, proclaiming the greatness of
God and his mercies toward men; words to prepare you for
today's great celebration of the Eucharist on the campus of
the University of Navarre.

   Consider for a moment the event I have just described. We
are celebrating the holy Eucharist, the sacramental sacrifice
of the Body and Blood of our Lord, that mystery of faith
which binds together all the mysteries of Christianity. We are
celebrating, therefore, the most sacred and transcendent act
which we, men and women, with God's grace can carry out
in this life: receiving the Body and Blood of our Lord is, in a
certain sense, like loosening our ties with earth and time, so
as to be already with God in Heaven, where Christ himself
will wipe the tears from our eyes and where there will be no
more death, nor mourning, nor cries of distress, because the
old world will have passed away.[1]

   This profound and consoling truth, which theologians
usually call the eschatological meaning of the Eucharist,
could, however, be misunderstood. Indeed, this has hap-

This homily was delivered at a Mass on the campus of the University of
Navarre, Spain; it has previously been published in *Conversations with
Monsignor [Josemaría] Escrivá.*

pened whenever people have tried to present the Christian way of life as something exclusively *spiritual*—or better, spiritualistic—something reserved for *pure*, extraordinary people who remain aloof from the contemptible things of this world, or at most tolerate them as something that the spirit just has to live alongside, while we are on this earth.

When people take this approach, churches become the setting *par excellence* of the Christian way of life. And being a Christian means going to church, taking part in sacred ceremonies, getting into an ecclesiastical mentality, in a special kind of *world*, considered the ante-chamber to Heaven, while the ordinary world follows its own separate course. In this case, Christian teaching and the life of grace would pass by, brushing very lightly against the turbulent advance of human history but never coming into proper contact with it.

On this October morning, as we prepare to enter upon the memorial of our Lord's Pasch, we *flatly reject* this deformed vision of Christianity. Reflect for a moment on the setting of our Eucharist, of our Act of Thanksgiving. We find ourselves in a unique temple; we might say that the nave is the University campus; the altarpiece, the University library; over there, the machinery for constructing new buildings; above us, the sky of Navarre. . . .

Surely this confirms in your minds, in a tangible and unforgettable way, the fact that everyday life is the true setting for your lives as Christians. Your daily encounter with Christ takes place where your fellow men, your yearnings, your work, and your affections are. It is in the midst of the most material things of the earth that we must sanctify ourselves, serving God and all mankind.

This I have been teaching all the time, using words from holy Scripture: the world is not evil, because it comes from the hands of God, because it is his creation, because Yahweh looked upon it and saw that it was good.[2] It is we ourselves,

52

men and women, who make it evil and ugly with our sins and unfaithfulness. Don't doubt it, my children: any attempt to escape from the noble reality of daily life is, for you men and women of the world, something opposed to the will of God.

On the contrary, you must realize now, more clearly than ever, that God is calling you to serve him *in and from* the ordinary, secular, and civil activities of human life. He waits for us everyday, in the laboratory, in the operating theatre, in the army barracks, in the university chair, in the factory, in the workshop, in the fields, in the home, and in all the immense panorama of work. Understand this well: there is *something* holy, something divine hidden in the most ordinary situations, and it is up to each one of you to discover it.

I often said to the university students and workers who were with me in the thirties that they had to know how to *materialize* their spiritual lives. I wanted to warn them of the temptation, so common then and now, to lead a kind of double life: on the one hand, an inner life, a life related to God; and on the other, as something separate and distinct, their professional, social, and family lives, made up of small earthly realities.

No, my children! We cannot lead a double life. We cannot have a split personality if we want to be Christians. There is only one life, made of flesh and spirit. And it is that life which has to become, in both body and soul, holy and filled with God: we discover the invisible God in the most visible and material things.

There is no other way, my daughters and sons: either we learn to find our Lord in ordinary, everyday life, or we shall never find him. That is why I tell you that our age needs to give back to matter and to the apparently trivial events of life their noble, original meaning. It needs to place them at the service of the kingdom of God; it needs to spiritualize them,

turning them into a means and an occasion for a continuous
meeting with Jesus Christ.

The genuine Christian approach—which professes the   53
resurrection of all flesh—has always quite logically opposed
"dis-incarnation," without fear of being judged materialistic.
We can, therefore, rightly speak of a *Christian materialism*,
which is boldly opposed to those materialisms which are
blind to the spirit.

What are the sacraments, which people in early times
described as the footprints of the Incarnate Word, if not the
clearest expression of this way which God has chosen in
order to sanctify us and to lead us to Heaven? Don't you see
that each sacrament is the love of God, with all its creative
and redemptive power, given to us through the medium of
material things? What is this Eucharist which we are about to
celebrate if not the Adorable Body and Blood of our Redeemer, which is offered to us through the lowly matter of
this world (wine and bread), through the elements of nature,
cultivated by man, as the recent Ecumenical Council has reminded us.[3]

It is understandable, my children, that the Apostle should
write: "All things are yours, you are Christ's and Christ is
God's."[4] We have here an ascending movement which the
Holy Spirit, poured into our hearts, wants to call forth in this
world: upward from the earth to the glory of the Lord. And to
make it clear that in such a movement everything is included,
even what seems most commonplace, Saint Paul also wrote:
"In eating, in drinking, do everything for God's glory."[5]

This doctrine of Sacred Scripture, as you know, is to be   54
found in the very core of the spirit of Opus Dei. It should lead
you to do your work perfectly, to love God and your fellow
men by putting love in the little things of everyday life, and
discovering that *divine something* which is hidden in small
details. The lines of a Castilian poet are especially appropriate

here: "Write slowly and with a careful hand, for doing things well is more important than doing them." [6]

I assure you, my children, that when a Christian carries out with love the most insignificant everyday action, that action overflows with the transcendence of God. That is why I have told you so often, and hammered away at it, that the Christian vocation consists in making heroic verse out of the prose of each day. Heaven and earth seem to merge, my children, on the horizon. But where they really meet is in your hearts, when you sanctify your everyday lives. . . .

I have just said, sanctify your everyday lives. And with these words I refer to the whole program of your task as Christians. Stop dreaming. Leave behind false idealisms, fantasies, and what I usually call *mystical wishful thinking*:* If only I hadn't married; if only I had a different job or qualification; if only I were in better health; if only I were younger; if only I were older. Instead, turn to the most material and immediate reality, which is where our Lord is: "Look at my hands and my feet," said the risen Jesus, "be assured that it is myself; touch me and see; a spirit has not flesh and bones, as you see that I have." [7]

Light is shed upon many aspects of the world in which you live, when you start from these truths. Take your activity as citizens, for instance. A man who knows that the world—and not just the Church—is the place where he finds Christ, loves that world. He endeavors to become properly trained, intellectually and professionally. He makes up his own mind, in full freedom, about the problems of the environment in which he moves, and he takes his own decisions in consequence. As the decisions of a Christian, they derive from personal reflection, which strives in all humility to grasp the

---

* A play on words between *ojalá* ("would that," "if only") and *hojalata* ("tin-plate"). *Mística ojalatera* is "tin-can mysticism," as well as "mystical wishful thinking."

will of God in both the unimportant and the important events of his life.

But it never occurs to such a Christian to think or say that he was stepping down from the temple into the world to represent the Church, or that his solutions are *the Catholic solutions* to the problems. That would be completely inadmissible! That would be clericalism, *official Catholicism*, or whatever you want to call it. In any case, it means doing violence to the very nature of things. What you must do is foster a real *lay mentality*, which will lead to three conclusions: —be honorable enough to shoulder your own personal responsibility; —be Christian enough to respect those brothers in the faith who, in matters of free discussion, propose solutions that differ from yours; and —be Catholic enough not to make a tool of our Mother the Church, involving her in human factions.

It is obvious that, in this field as in all others, you would not be able to carry out this program of sanctifying your everyday life if you did not enjoy all the freedom that proceeds from your dignity as men and women created in the image of God and that the Church freely recognizes. Personal freedom is essential for the Christian life. But do not forget, my sons, that I always speak of a responsible freedom.

Interpret, then, my words as what they are: a call to exercise your rights every day, and not just in times of emergency. A call to fulfill honorably your commitments as citizens in all fields—in politics and in financial affairs, in university life and in your job—accepting with courage all the consequences of your free decisions and shouldering the personal independence that is yours. A Christian *lay outlook* of this sort will enable you to flee from all intolerance, from all fanaticism. To put it positively, it will help you live in peace with all your fellow citizens, and to promote understanding and harmony in the various spheres of social life.

55

56   I know I have no need to remind you of something which I have been saying for so many years. This doctrine of civic freedom, of understanding, of living in harmony with other people, forms a very important part of the message spread by Opus Dei. Must I affirm once again that the men and women who want to serve Jesus Christ in the Work of God, are simply *citizens the same as everyone else*, who strive to live their Christian vocation to its ultimate consequences with a deep sense of responsibility?

Nothing distinguishes my children from their fellow citizens. On the other hand, apart from the faith they share, they have nothing in common with the members of religious congregations. I love the religious, and I venerate and admire their apostolates, their cloister, their separation from the world, their *contemptus mundi*, which are *other* signs of holiness in the Church. But the Lord has not given me a religious vocation, and for me to desire it would not be in order. No authority on earth can force me to be a religious, just as no authority can make me marry. I am a secular priest: a priest of Jesus Christ who is passionately in love with the world.

57   These are the men and women who have followed Jesus Christ in the company of this poor sinner: a small percentage of priests, who have previously exercised a secular profession or trade; a large number of secular priests from many dioceses throughout the world, who in this way confirm their obedience to their respective bishops, their love for their diocesan work, and the effectiveness of it. Their arms are always wide open, in the form of a cross, to make room in their hearts for all souls; and like myself they live in the hustle and bustle of the workaday world which they love. And finally, a great multitude made up of men and women of different nations, and tongues, and races, who earn their living with their work. Most of them are married, many others single; they share with their fellow citizens in the important task of making temporal society more human and more just. And they work, as I have said, shoulder to shoulder with their fellow men, experiencing with them successes and failures in the noble struggle of daily endeavor, as they strive to fulfill their duties and to exercise their social and civic rights. And all this with naturalness, like any other conscientious Christian, without considering themselves special. Blended into the mass of their companions, they try at the same time to detect the flashes of divine splendor that shine through the commonest everyday realities.

Similarly, the activities that are promoted by Opus Dei as an association have these eminently secular characteristics: they are not ecclesiastical activities—they do not in any way represent the hierarchy of the Church. They are the fruit of human, cultural, and social initiatives of ordinary citizens who try to make them reflect the light of the gospel and to bring them the warmth of Christ's love. An example that will help to make this clear is that Opus Dei does not, and never will, undertake the task of directing diocesan seminaries, in which bishops *instituted by the Holy Spirit*[8] train their future priests.

Opus Dei, on the other hand, does foster technical training 58 centers for industrial workers, agricultural training schools for farm laborers, centers for primary, secondary, and university education, and many other varied activities all over the world, because its apostolic zeal, as I wrote many years ago, is like a sea without shores.

But what need have I to speak at length on this topic, when your very presence here is more eloquent than a long address? You, Friends of the University of Navarre, are part of a body of people who know it is committed to the progress of the broader society to which it belongs. Your sincere encouragement, your prayers, sacrifices, and contributions are not offered on the basis of Catholic confessionalism. Your cooperation is a clear testimony of a well-formed social conscience, which is concerned with the temporal common good. You are witnesses to the fact that a university can be born of the energies of the people and be sustained by the people.

On this occasion, I want to offer my thanks once again for the cooperation lent to our University by my noble city of Pamplona, by the region of Navarre, by the Friends of the University from every part of Spain and—I say this with particular feeling—by people who are not Spaniards, even by people who are not Catholics or Christians, who have understood the purpose and spirit of this enterprise and have shown it with their active help.

Thanks to all of them this University has grown ever more effective as a focus of civic freedom, of intellectual training, of professional endeavor, and a stimulus for university education generally. Your generous sacrifice is part of the foundation of this whole undertaking, which seeks to promote the human sciences, social welfare, and the teaching of the faith.

What I have just pointed out has been clearly understood by the people of Navarre, who also recognize that their University is a factor in the economic development and, especially, in the social advancement of the region; a factor which has given so many of their children an opportunity to enter the intellectual professions that otherwise would have been difficult and, in some cases, impossible to obtain. This awareness of the role that the University would play in their lives is surely what inspired the support that Navarre has lent it from the beginning—support that will undoubtedly keep on growing in enthusiasm and extent.

I continue to harbor the hope—because it accords both with the requirements of justice and with the practice that obtains in so many countries—that the time will come when the Spanish government will contribute its share to lighten the burden of an undertaking that seeks no private profit but, on the contrary, is totally dedicated to the service of society and tries to work efficiently for the present and future prosperity of the nation.

And now, my sons and daughters, let me consider another   59 aspect of everyday life that is particularly dear to me. I refer to human love, to the noble love between a man and a woman, to courtship and marriage. I want to say once again that this holy human love is not something to be merely permitted or tolerated alongside the true activities of the spirit, as might be insinuated by those false spiritualisms which I referred to earlier. I have been preaching and writing just the very opposite for forty years, and now those who did not understand are beginning to grasp the point.

Love, which leads to marriage and family, can also be a marvelous divine way, a vocation, a path for a complete dedication to our God. Do things perfectly, I have reminded you. Put love into the little duties of each day; discover that *divine something* contained in these details. All this teaching has a special place in that area of life where human love has its setting.

All of you who are lecturers or students or who work in any capacity in the University of Navarre know that I have entrusted your love to Mary, Mother of Fair Love. And here, on the University campus, you have the shrine, which we built so devoutly, as a place to receive your prayers and the offering of that wonderful and pure love on which she bestows her blessing.

"Surely you know that your bodies are the shrines of the Holy Spirit, who is God's gift to you, so that you are no longer your own masters?" [9] How often, before the statue of the Blessed Virgin, of the Mother of Fair Love, will you not reply to the Apostle's question with a joyful affirmation: Yes, we know that this is so and we want to live it with your powerful help, O Virgin Mother of God.

Contemplative prayer will rise within you whenever you meditate on this impressive truth: something as material as my body has been chosen by the Holy Spirit as his dwelling place. . . . I no longer belong to myself. . . . My body and soul, my whole being, belong to God. . . . And this prayer will be rich in practical results arising from the great consequence which the Apostle himself suggests: "Glorify God in your bodies." [10]

60   Besides, you cannot fail to realize that only among those who understand and value in all its depth what we have just considered about human love can there arise another ineffable insight of which Jesus speaks:[11] an insight which is a pure gift of God, moving a person to surrender body and soul to the Lord, to offer him an undivided heart, without the mediation of earthly love.

61   I must finish now, my children. I said at the beginning that I wanted to tell you something of the greatness and mercy of God. I think I have done so in speaking to you about sanctifying your everyday life. A holy life in the midst of secular affairs, lived without fuss, with simplicity, with truthfulness: is this not today the most moving manifestation of the *magnalia Dei*,[12] of those prodigious mercies which God has always worked and still works, in order to save the world?

Now, with the Psalmist I ask you to join in my prayer and in my praise: *Magnificate Dominum mecum, et extollamus nomen eius simul*[13] — "Praise the Lord with me, let us extol his name together." In other words, my children, let us live by faith.

Let us take up the shield of faith, the helmet of salvation, and the sword of the Spirit, which is God's Word. That is what Saint Paul encourages us to do in the epistle to the Ephesians,[14] which was read in the liturgy a few moments ago.

Faith is a virtue which we Christians greatly need, and in a special way in this "Year of Faith," which our beloved Holy Father Pope Paul VI has decreed. For, without faith, we lack the very foundation for the sanctification of ordinary life.

A living faith in these moments, because we are drawing near to the *mysterium fidei*,[15] to the Holy Eucharist: because we are about to participate in our Lord's Pasch, which sums up and effects the mercies of God toward men.

Faith, my children, in order to acknowledge that within a few moments *the work of our Redemption*[16] is going to be renewed on this altar. Faith, to savor the Creed and to experience, around this altar and in this assembly, the presence of Christ, who makes us *cor unum et anima una*,[17] "one heart and one soul," and transforms us into a family, a Church which is one, holy, catholic, apostolic, and Roman, which for us is the same as saying universal.

Faith, finally, my beloved daughters and sons, to show the world that all this is not just ceremonies and words, but a divine reality, as we present to mankind the testimony of an ordinary life made holy, in the name of the Father and of the Son and of the Holy Spirit and of Holy Mary.

Epilogue
Getting to the Roots

By Alvaro del Portillo, Prelate of Opus Dei

The so called "practical" people are not really the most useful in the service of Christ's Church, nor are those who merely expound theories. Rather it is the true contemplatives who best serve her: those with the steady, generous, and passionate desire of transfiguring and divinizing all creation with Christ and in Christ. It may sound paradoxical, but in the Church of Jesus Christ, the mystic is the only truly practical person.

"To serve the Church without using the Church to serve yourself"; "to serve the Church as the Church wants to be served": this was the *driving passion* of the Servant of God, Josemaría Escrivá. The tenth anniversary of his death has evoked thoughts which I would like to express as a heartfelt token of gratitude and at the same time as a reminder of a lesson which I apply in the first place to myself. For his faithfulness in service to the Church has borne results that have been apparent to all, and they testify to the fact that only someone who seeks *extasis*—literally, going out of himself, spending himself fully and exclusively in the service of God and of souls—achieves authentic spiritual fruitfulness.

What the founder of Opus Dei was so consumed with, he expressed in a phrase which sounds like one of those heraldic mottoes: *Para servir, servir* (in order to serve, serve)— that is, to be useful, you ought to have a spirit of service and show it with deeds. The only honor he ever sought was to serve the Church. The only right was to renounce all rights except that of offering himself in a constant and total sacrifice of prayer and work.

An instrument, no matter how ordinary it may be, is really effective only if it is ordered to its true purpose: "First, prayer; then, atonement; in the third place—very much 'in the third place'—action." [1] What makes the spirituality of Opus Dei so pragmatic is precisely that its principal characteristic, which the Servant of God wrote in blazing letters, is to immerse contemplation directly into everyday life, in a constant search for intimacy with God in the midst of the dense fabric of secular work.

For this pioneer of lay spirituality, the first effect of living the presence of God in one's work is the improvement of the quality of that work even in its technical aspects. If work is to be of specific and vital service to the living Body of Christ, it must first of all be well done. All sloppiness, carelessness, frivolity, and superficiality have to be totally rejected, since they detract from the dignity of that service which any work implies.

The supernatural purpose, therefore, is not a stamp that is put on man's work without affecting its intrinsic quality. It is not a label, which may take the merchandise to its destination, but without really touching it and regardless of whether it is sound or faulty. Contemplation has a corrective effect on an action whenever that action does not achieve a standard proper to the dignity of a human being or the even higher standard proper to children of God, or when it fails to build up the People of God.

This becomes the fountain from which the daily life of a Christian flows. It is a stream in whose waters his love is constantly refreshed, as it seeks the Beloved through city streets and squares, across seas, through sown fields and on craggy peaks. This fountain and this stream expand the mind and enlarge the heart, leading them to breathe with new

fervor the free air of that *sentire cum Ecclesia*. Few things
the founder of Opus Dei detested so much as the nearsighted-
ness of those who never see anything beyond their own
selfish interests, the meanness of the individualist and of a
bourgeois outlook, and the rickets of an *esprit de corps*. "May
I never see 'cliques' developing in your work. It would make
a mockery of the apostolate: for if, in the end, the 'clique' got
control of a universal undertaking, how quickly that universal
undertaking would be reduced to a clique itself!"[2]

Only the contemplative soul knows how to beat continu-
ously in unison with the whole Church. It alone can sustain
fidelity to its own vocation as it responds correctly and precisely to each service it is asked to give. Only such a soul
realizes, from its own experience, that the Spirit "blows
where it wills, and you hear the sound of it, but you do not
know whence it comes or whither it goes."[3] It also knows
that in this world of confusion and relativism there is only
one place of which it can always and with absolute certainty
be said: "Here is the spirit of Jesus": it is in the Church. *Ubi
ecclesia, ibi spiritus Domini; ubi Spiritus Domini, ibi
ecclesia et omnis gratia* (Saint Irenaeus)—"Where the
Church is, there is the Spirit of the Lord; where the spirit of
the Lord is, there is the Church and all grace."

That is why those who are inspired by the Holy Spirit to
carry out a divine enterprise *currunt ad Ecclesiam*—"go run-
ning to the Church"—to use another expression of Saint
Irenaeus. The individual's inner conviction of the details contained in the call he has received has the seal of an authentic
charism only if he is convinced that it is by working in the
Church, and with the Church, that one is living and acting
with the Spirit of God.

Ever since October 2, 1928, Monsignor Escrivá was abso-
lutely sure that Opus Dei was truly from God, that it was "an
imperative command of Christ." Those intimate graces which

ascetical and mystical theology deal with—divine touches, interior locutions and the like—are of a kind that cannot be shaken by anyone or anything. But even after *seeing* God's will for Opus Dei a mission entrusted exclusively to him, Monsignor Escrivá sought from the very beginning to be fully united to the hierarchy of the Church. He did not want to take a single step without its approval and blessing. He established specific norms for the Work so that always and everywhere it would proceed in close union with the aims of the local Churches. With disarming simplicity he affirmed that he loved Opus Dei to the extent that it served the Church. How often have I heard him say: "If Opus Dei does not serve the Church, I am not interested in it!"

God sometimes asks founders to make the sacrifice of Abraham. Abraham's whole life was focused on his only son, in whom the promise was to be fulfilled. He was to become the father of a great people, more numerous than the stars in the sky or the sands of the desert. . . . And then suddenly God demands the offering, the total sacrifice. There were two moments in the life of the founder of Opus Dei which put his supernatural spirit to the test of pure faith. Both had to do with this service to the Church; for love of the Church is the touchstone of the truly Christian soul, which, according to Saint Ambrose, is always an "ecclesiastical soul."

The first of these harsh trials took place in Madrid on Thursday, June 22, 1933, on the eve of the Feast of the Sacred Heart. The note in which he himself tells of it has all the chilling sensation of truth, written, as it was, in his own hand and so soon after the event: "Alone, on a balcony of this church of Perpetual Succour, I was trying to pray before Jesus in the Blessed Sacrament exposed in the monstrance, when, for an instant and without formulating any reasons—there are none—there came to my mind this most bitter thought: 'And what if it is all a lie, an illusion of yours . . . , and you are wasting your time . . . and, what is worse, you are making others waste theirs?

"It was a matter of seconds, but how much suffering it caused! Then I spoke to Jesus, and I told him: 'Lord, if the Work is not yours, destroy it. If it is yours, confirm me.'

"Immediately, I not only felt confirmed in the truth of his will regarding the Work, but I saw clearly a point of its organization, which until then I did not know at all how to resolve."

The second trial was similar to the first, and its context was a storm that had been unleashed against the founder and against Opus Dei in the early forties. The Work had just been canonically born, so to speak. The bishop had granted the first written approval on March 19, 1941, precisely to stop the painful campaign aimed at discrediting Opus Dei even in Rome. On September 25, 1941, the Servant of God was in the Spanish town of La Granja de San Ildefonso, not far from Segovia. He was exhausted. In addition to the suffering occasioned by these sad events, there was the fatigue caused by the apostolate he was carrying on throughout the length and breadth of Spain—preaching retreats to priests and sowing the seed of the Work in every kind of milieu. That day he wrote me a letter. I quote some of its more significant lines:

"Alvaro, may Jesus watch over you for me. . . . Yesterday I celebrated Mass for the local Ordinary, and today I have offered the Holy Sacrifice and everything during the day for the Supreme Pontiff, for the person of the Pope and for his intentions. After the Consecration, I certainly felt an interior impulse compelling me to do something which cost me tears. Completely convinced at the same time that the Pope has to love the Work very much, and while looking at Jesus in the Eucharist, there on the corporal, with tears burning in my eyes, with my heart I told him truly: 'Lord, if you want, I accept *the injustice.*' You can figure out what *the injustice* is—the destruction of all of *God's work*. I know that I pleased him. How could I refuse making this act of union with his will, if he was asking it of me? Once before, in 1933 or 1934, at a price he alone knows, I did the same thing.

"My son, what a beautiful harvest the Lord is preparing for us once our Holy Father gets to know us truly and not through calumnies, and learns about us as we really are, his most faithful children, and blesses us! I feel like shouting out—and without worrying what others may say—that cry which has sometimes come to my lips while preaching to you: O Jesus! What a harvest!"

His love for the Church and the Pope sustained him and impressed on his soul an unshakeable confidence at the most difficult moments. He offered his life daily for the whole Holy Church and for the Holy Father—frequently adding, "and a thousand lives if I had them." Following his example, many souls from all sorts of countries and cultures have sought the strength to put no limits on their self-sacrifice. They have tried to carry out their daily work with a smile on their lips in the desire of spending their lives in unconditional service to Christ's Spouse. The words for private devotion to the Servant of God effectively express that aspiration: "Grant that I also may learn to turn all the circumstances and events of my life into opportunities to love you and to serve the Church, the Pope, and all souls, with joy and simplicity, lighting up the paths of the earth with faith and love."

Notes

Prologue: Josemaría Escrivá's Love for the Church

1. Josemaría Escrivá, *Christ Is Passing By*, 44.
2. Josemaría Escrivá, *Letter*, March 24, 1930.
3. Josemaría Escrivá, *The Way*, 291.
4. Josemaría Escrivá, *Letter*, March 19, 1954.
5. *Lumen gentium*, no. 40.
6. Ibid.
7. Ibid, no. 42.
8. See, among others: Cardinal J. Frings, *Fuer die Menschen bestellt* (Cologne, 1973), pp. 149–150; Cardinal Sebastiano Baggio, *Avvenire* (Milan, 1975); Cardinal Sergio Pignedoli, *Scepter Booklet 41*; Cardinal Marcelo Gonzalez Martin, *Los domingos de ABC* (Madrid, 1975); Cardinal Franz Koenig, *Corriere della Sera* (Milan, 1975); Cardinal Mario Casariego, Homily at ordination of fifty-four members of Opus Dei, in *L'Osservatore Romano* (July 1975); etc.
9. Josemaría Escrivá, *Consideraciones espirituales* (Madrid, 1934), p. 94.
10. Mt 5:14.
11. Tob 12:7.
12. Mt 25:23.
13. *Lumen gentium*, no. 4.
14. *Presbyterorum ordinis*, no. 2.
15. Josemaría Escrivá, *Letter*, March 11, 1940.
16. *Christ Is Passing By*, 2.
17. Vatican Council II, Decree *Apostolicam actuositatem*, no. 2.
18. Ibid.; *Lumen gentium*, no. 33; *Apostolicam actuositatem*, no. 3; Decree, *Ad gentes*, no. 15.
19. *Lumen gentium*, no. 17.
20. Josemaría Escrivá, *Conversations with Monsignor Escrivá*, 21.
21. *Apostolicam actuositatem*, no. 2.
22. Vatican Council II, Pastoral Constitution *Gaudium et spes*, no. 34.
23. *Conversations*, 10.
24. *Christ Is Passing By*, 105.
25. Josemaría Escrivá, *Letter*, March 11, 1940.
26. *Conversations*, 114.
27. Josemaría Escrivá, *Letter*, May 31, 1943.
28. Josemaría Escrivá, *Letter*, March 19, 1954.
29. Josemaría Escrivá, *The Way*, 353.
30. *Lumen gentium*, no. 31; *Apostolicam actuositatem*, nos. 11–14; *Ad gentes*, no. 21.
31. *Apostolicam actuositatem*, no. 24.
32. *Gaudium et spes*, no. 43.
33. Josemaría Escrivá, *Letter*, January 9, 1932.
34. *Gaudium et spes*, no. 43.
35. *Christ Is Passing By*, 99.
36. *Conversations*, 116–117.
37. Eph 5:32.
38. *The Way*, 27.
39. *Christ Is Passing By*, 23.

40. *Gaudium et spes*, no. 48.
41. *Christ Is Passing By*, no. 30.
42. *Presbyterorum ordinis*, no. 2.
43. Josemaría Escrivá, *Letter*, February 2, 1945.
44. *Presbyterorum ordinis*, no. 3.
45. Ibid., no. 6.
46. *Christ Is Passing By*, 99.
47. *Presbyterorum ordinis*, no. 3.
48. Ibid., no. 6.
49. Ibid., no. 8.
50. Ibid., no. 14.
51. Ibid., no. 18.
52. Ibid., no. 13.
53. *Lumen gentium*, no. 41.
54. *Conversations*, 22.
55. Ibid.
56. *Lumen gentium*, no. 17.
57. 1 Tim 2:4.

Loyalty to the Church

1. See Ps 17:19-20, 2-3; Introit of the Mass.
2. Prayer, Mass of the Second Sunday after Pentecost.
3. Ps 119:1, 2; Ps 7:2, Gradual of the Mass.
4. Jn 10:8, 10.
5. Lk 14:23.
6. Saint Thomas Aquinas, *Summa theologiae*, III, q. 64, a. 2, ad 3.
7. Nicene-Constantinopolitan Creed, Denzinger-Schön. 150 (86).
8. Pius IX, *Letter of the Holy Office to the Bishops of England*, September 16, 1864, Denzinger-Schön. 2888 (1686).
9. Vatican Council II, Dogmatic Constitution *Lumen gentium*, no. 8.
10. Jn 17:11.
11. Jn 17:21.
12. Mt 12:25.
13. Jn 10:16.
14. Jn 15:1-5.
15. Saint Cyprian, *De catholicae*

Ecclesiae unitate, 6 (PL 4, 503).
16. Saint John Chrysostom, *Homilia de capto Eutropio*, 6.
17. Vatican Council I, *Dogmatic Constitution on the Church*, Denzinger-Schön. 3070 (1836).
18. Saint Cyprian, *De catholicae Ecclesiae unitate*, 6 (PL 4, 503).
19. Eph 4:4-6.
20. Eph 5:25-27.
21. Mt 16:18.
22. 1 Pet 2:9.
23. Sir 17:31.
24. Pius XII, encyclical *Mystici corporis*, June 29, 1943.
25. Ibid.
26. Mt 28:20.
27. *Summa theologiae*, III, q. 64, a. 6, ad 2.
28. Mt 13:47.
29. 1 Tim 2:4-6.
30. Saint Cyril, *Catechesis*, 18, 23.
31. *Summa theologiae*, III, q. 60, a. 5.
32. Ibid., q. 62, a. 1, ad 1.
33. Vatican Council II, *Constitutiones, Decreta, Declarationes* (Vatican 1966), p. 1079.
34. Saint Ambrose, *In XII Ps enarratio*, 40, 30.
35. Mt 28:18-20.
36. Jn 15:16.
37. Council of Trent, *Doctrine on the Sacrament of Holy Orders*, Denzinger-Schön. 1768 (960).
38. Mt 16:18.
39. Lk 22:32.
40. Vatican Council I, *Dogmatic Constitution*, Denzinger-Schön. 3059 (1826).
41. Pius IX, *Letter of the Holy Office*, Denzinger-Schön. 2888 (1686).
42. *Summa theologiae*, III, q. 68, a. 9, ad 2.
43. Ibid., ad 1.

44. Ibid., q. 22, a. 4.
45. Saint Thomas Aquinas, *In IV Sent.*, d. 13, q. 1, a 1.
46. See Acts 8:26-40.
47. See Acts 10:1-48.
48. See Acts 13:6-12.
49. Mt 20:6-7.
50. Jn 5:7.
51. Saint Augustine, *Enarrationes in psalmos*, 70, 2, 12.

The Supernatural Aim of the Church

1. Saint Cyprian, *De oratione dominica*, 23 (PL 4, 553).
2. Saint Augustine, *Enchiridion*, 56, 15 (PL 40, 259).
3. Creed of the Mass.
4. Saint John Damascene, *Adversum Iconium*, 12 (PG 96, 1358).
5. See Mt 28:20.
6. Leo XIII, encyclical *Divinum illud munus*, AAS 29, p. 648: *Ecclesia, quae iam concepta, ex latere ipso secundi Adami velut in cruce dormientis orta erat, sese in lucem hominum insigni modo primitus dedit die celeberrima Pentecostes. Ipsaque die beneficia sua Spiritus Sanctus in mystico Christi Corpore prodere coepit.*
7. Dt 32:10.
8. Paul VI, Address, June 23, 1966.
9. Saint Augustine, *Enarrationes in psalmos*, 103, 2, 5 (PL 37, 1353).
10. Eph 4:11-12.
11. Rom 12:5.
12. Col 1:18.
13. Saint Augustine, *Enarrationes in psalmos*, 56, 1 (PL 36, 662).
14. Leo XIII, encyclical *Satis cognitum*, AAS 28, p. 710.
15. Ibid., p. 724.
16. Ibid, pp. 712-713.
17. Eph 1:22-23.
18. Eph 1:10.
19. Eph 1:4.
20. 1 Tim 2:4.
21. Jn 20:21.
22. Mt 28:18-20.
23. Mk 16:16.
24. Origen, *In Iesu nave homilia*, 5, 3 (PG 12, 841).
25. Saint Cyprian, *De catholicae Ecclesiae unitate*, 6 (PL 4, 503).
26. Saint Augustine, *Sermo ad Cassariensis ecclesiae plebem*, 6 (PL 43, 456).
27. Pius XII, encyclical *Humani generis*, AAS 42, p. 570.
28. Pius XII, *Letter from the Holy Office to the Archbishop of Boston*, Denziger-Schön. 3868.
29. Council of Trent, *De iustificatione*, chap. 4, Denziger-Schön. 1524.
30. *Summa theologiae*, III, q. 68, a. 2.
31. Pius IX, encyclical *Quanto conficiamur moerore*, August 10, 1863, Denziger-Schön. 1677 (2866).
32. See *Summa theologiae*, III, q. 62, a. 1.
33. See ibid., q. 61, a. 2.
34. 2 Tim 4:1-4.
35. See Lk 10:42.
36. Mt 15:8.
37. See Is 58:1.
38. Acts 4:11-12.
39. Saint Augustine, *Enarrationes in psalmos*, 88, 2, 14 (PL 37, 1140).
40. Saint Cyprian, *De catholicae Ecclesiae unitate*, 6 (PL 4, 502).
41. Vatican Council II, Dogmatic Constitution *Lumen gentium*, no. 8.
42. Ibid., no. 18.
43. See Rom 8:21.
44. Rom 11:33-36.
45. Mt 28:19.

A Priest Forever
1. Ps 22:1; Communion Antiphon, Mass for Saturday in the Fourth Week of Lent.
2. Ps 15:5.
3. 1 Cor 4:1.
4. 1 Pet 2:9–10.
5. Eph 1:3–4.
6. See Rom 13:12.
7. Saint Catherine of Siena, *Dialogues*, chap. 116; see Ps 104:15.
8. Vatican Council II, Constitution *Sacrosanctum Concilium*, no. 7; see Council of Trent, *Doctrine on the Sacrifice of the Mass*, chap. 2.
9. Saint Gregory the Great, *Dialogue*, 4, 59.
10. 1 Cor 4:7.
11. Vatican Council II, Decree *Presbyterorum ordinis*, no. 2.
12. Council of Trent, *Doctrine on the Sacrament of Order*, chap. 1, Denziger-Schön. 1764 (957).
13. Vatican Council II, Dogmatic Constitution *Lumen gentium*, no. 10.
14. See Vatican Council II, Decree *Presbyterorum ordinis*, no. 6.
15. See *Presbyterorum ordinis*, no. 13.
16. Ibid.
17. Council of Trent, *Doctrine on the Most Holy Sacrifice of the Mass*, Denziger-Schön. 1743 (940).
18. *Lumen gentium*, no. 50.
19. Saint Thomas, *Summa theologiae suppl.* q. 36, a. 2, ad 1.
20. Deut 6:13; Mt 4:10.
21. See Col 1:24.

Passionately Loving the World
1. See Rev 21:4.
2. See Gen 1:7ff.
2. See Vatican Council II, Pastoral Constitution *Gaudium et spes*, no. 38.
4. 1 Cor 3:22–23.
5. 1 Cor 10:31.
6. A. Machado, *Poesías Completas*, *CLXI—Proverbios y cantares. XXIV* (Madrid: Espasa-Calpe, 1940): *Despacito, y buena letra: el hacer las cosas bien importa más que el hacerlas.*
7. Lk 24:39.
8. Acts 20:28.
9. 1 Cor 6:19.
10. 1 Cor 6:20.
11. Mt 19:11.
12. Sir 18:4.
13. Ps 33:4.
14. Eph 6:11ff.
15. 1 Tim 3:9.
16. Prayer over the Offerings, Mass of the Ninth Sunday after Pentecost.
17. Acts 4:32.

Epilogue: Getting to the Roots
1. Josemaría Escrivá, *The Way*, 82.
2. Ibid., 963.
3. Jn 3:8.

Index

Keyed to margin numbers in text

About the Author

Josemaría Escrivá de Balaguer was born in Barbastro, Spain, on January 9, 1902, the second of six children of Jose and Dolores Escrivá. Growing up in a devout family and attending Catholic schools, he learned the basic truths of the faith. Frequent confession and Communion, praying the Rosary, and almsgiving were a regular part of his childhood. The death of three younger sisters and his father's bankruptcy after business reverses taught him the meaning of suffering and brought maturity to his outgoing and cheerful temperament. In 1915, the family moved to Logroño, where his father had found new employment.

Beginning in 1918, Josemaría sensed that God was asking something of him. In order to be available for whatever God wanted of him, he began to study for the priesthood, first in Logroño and later in Saragossa. He was ordained a priest and began his pastoral ministry in 1925.

In 1927, Fr. Josemaría moved to Madrid to study for a graduate degree in law. He was accompanied by his mother, sister, and brother, as his father had died in 1924, and he was now head of the family. They were not well-off, and to support them he tutored law students. At the same time, he was active in pastoral work, especially among the poor and sick and with young children. To this work he enlisted manual workers, professional people, and university students so that they might learn the practical meaning of charity and their Christian responsibility to society.

On October 2, 1928, while making a retreat in Madrid, he understood his specific mission: he was to establish an institution within the Church dedicated to helping people in all walks of life to follow Christ, to seek holiness in their daily life, and to grow in love for God and their fellow men and women. This was the beginning of Opus Dei. He then dedicated all his strength to fulfilling this mission, certain that God had raised up Opus Dei to serve the Church. In 1930, he started Opus Dei's apostolic work with women, making clear that they had the same responsibility as men to serve society and the Church.

In 1934, he saw published his first collection of short points for prayer and reflection, under the title *Spiritual Considerations* (later translated into English as *The Way*). Expanded and revised, it has gone through many editions; more than four million copies in many different languages are now in print. His other spiritual writings include *Holy Rosary*; *The Way of the Cross*; two collections of homilies, *Christ Is Passing By* and *Friends of God*; and *Furrow* and *The Forge*, which, like *The Way*, are books for prayer and reflection.

The development of Opus Dei began among young people. Its growth, however, was seriously impeded by the religious persecution and other hardships inflicted on the Catholic Church during the Spanish Civil War (1936–1939). Fr. Josemaría himself suffered severe hardships under this persecution. After the war, he traveled throughout Spain giving retreats to priests at the request of their bishops. Opus Dei gradually spread from Madrid to several other Spanish cities, and when World War II ended, in 1945, it took root also in other countries. Although the Work always had the approval of the local bishops, its then-unfamiliar message of personal holiness in the world met with some misunderstandings and suspicions—which Fr. Escrivá bore with great patience and charity.

While celebrating Mass in 1943, he received a new foundational grace to establish the Priestly Society of the Holy Cross, making it possible for some of Opus Dei's laymen to be ordained as priests. The full incorporation of both lay faithful and priests in Opus Dei, which makes a seamless cooperation in the apostolic work possible, is an essential feature of the foundational charism of Opus Dei, affirmed by the Church in granting Opus Dei the canonical status of a personal Prelature. In addition, the Priestly Society conducts activities, with the approval of the local bishops, for the spiritual development of diocesan priests and seminarians. Diocesan priests can also be part of the Priestly Society.

Aware that God meant Opus Dei to be part of the mission of the universal Church, Fr. Escrivá moved to Rome in 1946. By 1950, the Work had received pontifical approvals affirming its main foundational features—spreading the message of holiness in daily life; service to the Pope, the universal Church, and the particular churches; secularity and naturalness; fostering personal freedom and responsibility; and a pluralism consistent with Catholic moral, political, and social teachings.

In 1948, full membership in Opus Dei was opened to married people. Two years later, the Holy See approved the idea of accepting non-Catholics and even non-Christians as cooperators in the Work—persons who assist Opus Dei in its projects and programs without becoming members. The next decade saw Opus Dei launching a wide range of undertakings of manifestly Christian inspiration: professional schools, agricultural training centers, universities, primary and secondary schools, and hospitals and clinics, open to people of all races, religions, and social backgrounds.

During Vatican Council II (1962–1965), now-Monsignor Escrivá worked closely with many of the Council fathers, discussing such themes as the universal call to holiness and the importance of the laity in the mission of the Church. He did everything possible to implement the Council's teachings in the formative activities offered by Opus Dei throughout the world.

Between 1970 and 1975, Monsignor Escrivá undertook catechetical trips throughout Europe and Latin America, speaking about love of God, the sacraments, Christian dedication, and the need to sanctify work and family life. By the time of his death, Opus Dei had spread to thirty nations on six continents. Now it has members in sixty countries, and their numbers have increased to more than 84,000.

Monsignor Escrivá's death in Rome came suddenly on June 26, 1975, at age 73. Large numbers of bishops and ordinary faithful petitioned the Vatican to begin the process of investigating the sanctity of this remarkable priest. On May 17, 1992, Pope John Paul II declared him Blessed before a huge crowd in St. Peter's Square. The date of his canonization—the Church's formal declaration that Josemaría Escrivá is a saint—is October 6, 2002.

Publisher's Note

In Love with the Church brings together four homilies of Monsignor Josemaría Escrivá. The first three were originally published separately in booklet form. The fourth, "Passionately Loving the World," was first published in the collection titled *Conversations with Monsignor Escrivá* (1974). It is included also in this volume because it provides a magnificent meditation on how ordinary lay men and women can serve the Church. The Prologue and Epilogue of this present collection were originally published as articles written by Alvaro del Portillo, Prelate of Opus Dei, and are included here as further witness to Monsignor Escrivá's love for the Church.